I0819860

Tribalism’s Troubles

Responding to Rowan Williams

THE KAPUNDA PRESS

General Editor: Damien Freeman

PM Glynn Institute, Australian Catholic University

CHALICE OF LIBERTY:

PROTECTING RELIGIOUS FREEDOM IN AUSTRALIA

Frank Brennan – M. A. Casey – Greg Craven

TODAY'S TYRANTS: RESPONDING TO DYSON HEYDON

J. D. Heydon – Frank Brennan – Anne Henderson – Paul Kelly – M. A. Casey – Peter Kurti – M. J. Crennan
Hayden Ramsay – Shireen Morris – Michael Ondaatje – Sandra Lynch – Catherine Renshaw

FEDERATION'S MAN OF LETTERS:

PATRICK MCMAHON GLYNN

Anne Henderson – Anne Twomey – Suzanne Rutland – Patrick Mullins – John Fahey – Peter Boyce

NONSENSE ON STILTS:

RESCUING HUMAN RIGHTS IN AUSTRALIA

M. A. Casey – Damien Freeman – Catherine Renshaw – Tim Wilson
Nicholas Aroney – Emma Dawson – Terri Butler – Jennifer Cook – Bryan Turner

THE MARKET'S MORALS: RESPONDING TO JESSE NORMAN

Jesse Norman – Marc Stears – Greg Melleuish – Adrian Pabst – Amanda Walsh – Parnell McGuinness
Michael Easson – David Corbett – Tom Switzer – Cris Abbu – Tanya Aspland – Leanne Smith
M. A. Casey

STORY OF OUR COUNTRY: LABOR'S VISION FOR AUSTRALIA

Adrian Pabst

THE NEW SOCIAL CONTRACT: RENEWING THE LIBERAL VISION FOR AUSTRALIA

Tim Wilson

Forthcoming:

FAITH'S PLACE: DEMOCRACY IN A RELIGIOUS WORLD

Bryan S. Turner – Damien Freeman – Dean Smith – Luke Gosling – Ursula Stephens
Jocelyne Cesari – Jim Franklin – Robert Hefner – Riaz Hassan – David Saperstein – M. A. Casey

HOPE IN COMMON: RESTORING CONFIDENCE IN DEMOCRACY

Scott Stephens – Adrian Pabst – Damien Freeman – Julian Leeser
Alda Balthrop-Lewis – Richard Colledge – Karen Jones
Suzanne Killmister – Luke Bretherton – M. A. Casey

TRIBALISM'S TROUBLES

RESPONDING TO ROWAN WILLIAMS

EDITED BY
DAMIEN FREEMAN

CONNOR COURT PUBLISHING PTY LTD

PO Box 7257

Redland Bay QLD 4165

sales@connorcourt.com www.connorcourt.com

Cover image: Detail from a wall painting, Drake House, Melbourne (St Patrick's) Campus, Australian Catholic University.

ISBN:9781922449122

Cover design by Ian James

Printed in Australia

"After this I beheld, and, lo, a great multitude, which no man could number, of all nations, and tribes, and people, and tongues, stood before the throne, and before the Lamb, clothed with white robes, and palms in their hands . . ."

Revelation 7:9

Contents

Foreword

Margaret Beazley

It is uncontroversial to observe that in the recent history of governments in modern democracies 'identity politics' does not always well serve those who should be served well—the people. In the 2019 PM Glynn Lecture, 'Overcoming Political Tribalism', presented on 8 September 1019 at Australian Catholic University, North Sydney, the former Archbishop of Canterbury, Rowan Williams, carefully, gently, and eruditely exposes the demeaning aspects of modern tribalism, a product of an 'Enlightenment mindset' as a prelude to an analysis of modern political tribalism. His analysis leads him to a conclusion which, whilst not inevitable, is sufficiently foreboding as to require the Western world to take notice. As Williams observes, "a political debate in which your opponent is not merely mistaken, unwise, or uninformed, but malignant and/or subrational . . . slips readily into majoritarian tyranny".

Equally as carefully, gently, and eruditely, Williams proposes a solution to this near inevitability. He argues for a process of 'learning' from the 'other'. This in turn requires the creation of a 'shared language' to enable learning to occur. Williams turns to religious discourse as an exemplification of learning which eschews finality, and, therefore, rigidity of thought, but which embraces the 'learning journey'.

To characterize Williams's unravelling of modern tribalism as 'gentle' and 'erudite', is more a statement of the character of Williams himself. His analysis of tribalism, and political tribalism in particular, is no mere plea for civility. It hits hard and directly at its subject matter. It exposes a political process in modern Western democracies that has increasingly become fixated on exclusion and belittlement of the 'other'. It is intellectually challenging and thought-provoking. Whilst Williams would undoubtedly embrace those in agreement with him, the openness for which he advocates provides an environment in which questions can be raised, doubts can be explored, and different views can be expressed.

The responding essays are written in the context of this open environment. The authors of the twelve essays published in this book explore and critique Williams's thinking across a range of contemporary societal issues. The essays are a rich resource of contemporary thinking, making a significant contribution to learning on societal issues which call for deeper understanding and thoughtful discussion by all of us.

The 2019 PM Glynn lecture presented by Rowan Williams is the Institute's third lecture on Religion, Law and Public Life. The PM Glynn Institute is to be congratulated for providing this forum in which open, intellectual, thought-provoking discussion on contemporary societal issues can occur. The editor is to be congratulated for his curation of the responding essays, continuing the 'tradition', fostered by the PM Glynn Institute, of enabling the respectful exchange of ideas between lay scholars, public figures, and commentators who so ably contribute to 'thinking' in a modern society.

The Honourable Margaret Beazley AC QC
Governor of New South Wales
6 July 2020

Introduction

Damien Freeman

The Buttington Oak, which fell in February 2018, is thought to have been planted a thousand years earlier near Offa's Dyke, on the border of England and Wales, to mark the site of the Battle of Buttington, in which an allied host of Mercian, Wessex, and Welsh forces defeated the invading Vikings in 893. It had lived quietly since then; unnoticed until its 'rediscovery' in 2009. The oak is described as a 'working tree' that was pollarded to provide timber, which might have been fashioned into weapons for the local community. It was reckoned the second largest tree (but the largest by girth) in Wales. Apparently, it seemed remarkable, in some circles, that it survived for a millennium despite not being protected by any legislation.

It would be nice to think that the image on the dust jacket covering this volume depicts an immature Buttington Oak as it might have appeared in less peaceful times. A wild boar is depicted beneath the tree. It is being hunted by three dogs, one of which it has already killed. We know that the dogs belong to an unseen master because each has a collar around its neck. If such violent—perhaps even tribal—pursuits once took place under the tree, they are now long forgotten. Like a great and ancient oak, Lord Williams of Oystermouth has quietly witnessed the violence and tribal conflict that has gone on around him. It is to be hoped that, unlike the

Buttington Oak, his work—inspired by his motto, *the worship of God is the wisdom of man*—will serve a community that beats its wooden spears into pruning hooks long after the hunt has passed.

The Right Reverend and Right Honourable Rowan Douglas Williams was born on 14 June 1950 in Swansea, South Wales, into the Welsh-speaking family of the engineer, Aneurin Williams, and his wife, Nancy Delphine (née Morris). He was educated at Dynevor Secondary Grammar School, and then at Christ's College, Cambridge. He studied for his doctorate at Christ Church and Wadham College, Oxford, working on the Russian Orthodox theologian, Vladimir Lossky.

From 1975 to 1977, Dr Williams was a lecturer at the College of the Resurrection in Mirfield, West Yorkshire, and subsequently served as tutor and director of studies at Westcott House in Cambridge. In 1983, he was appointed to a University lectureship in divinity at the University of Cambridge. The following year, he was elected a Fellow of Clare College, Cambridge, and during his time at Clare he was arrested and fined for singing psalms as part of the Campaign for Nuclear Disarmament protest at Lakenheath airbase. At the age of thirty-six, he returned to the University of Oxford as Lady Margaret Professor of Divinity for six years from 1986.

He had been ordained as a deacon in Ely Cathedral in 1977, and subsequently as a priest in 1978, serving as curate at St George's, Chesterton, from 1980, then as Dean of Clare College, Cambridge, and residentiary canon of Christ Church, Oxford. In 1992, he was consecrated as Bishop of Monmouth, and was elected Archbishop of Wales in 2000.

He served as the one hundred and fourth Lord Archbishop of Canterbury, Primate of All England, and Metropolitan from 2002 until 2012.

Upon his retirement from the see of Canterbury, he became

the thirty-fifth Master of Magdalene College, Cambridge, and an honorary professor of contemporary Christian thought in the University of Cambridge. In 2013, he was elevated to the peerage as Baron Williams of Oystermouth, in the City and County of Swansea, and he sits in the House of Lords as a crossbencher.

He is the author of a multitude of books, including *The Wound of Knowledge* (1979), *Resurrection: Interpreting the Easter Gospel* (1982), *Eucharistic Sacrifice: The Roots of a Metaphor* (1982), *The Truce of God* (1983), *Peacemaking Theology* (1984), *Open to Judgement: Sermons and Addresses* (1984 and 1994), *Politics and Theological Identity* (with David Nicholls, 1984), *Christianity and the Ideal of Detachment* (1989), *Faith in the University* (1989), *After Silent Centuries* (1994), *On Christian Theology* (2000), *Christ on Trial* (2000), *Arius: Heresy and Tradition* (2nd edition, 2001), *The Poems of Rowan Williams* (2002), *Writing in the Dust: Reflections on 11th September and Its Aftermath* (2002), *Ponder These Things: Praying With Icons of the Virgin* (2002), *Faith and Experience in Early Monasticism* (2002), *Silence and Honey Cakes: The Wisdom of the Desert* (2003), *Teresa of Avila* (2003), *Lost Icons: Essays on Cultural Bereavement* (2003), *The Dwelling of the Light: Praying with Icons of Christ* (2003), *Darkness Yielding* (2004), *Anglican Identities* (2004), *Why Study the Past?* (2005), *Grace and Necessity: Reflections on Art and Love* (2005), *Tokens of Trust: An introduction to Christian belief* (2007), *Where God Happens: Discovering Christ in One Another* (2007), *Dostoevsky: Language, Faith and Fiction* (2008), *Choose Life* (2009), *Faith in the Public Square* (2012), *The Lion's World: A Journey into the Heart of Narnia* (2012), *Meeting God in Mark* (2014), *Being Christian: Baptism, Bible, Eucharist, Prayer* (2014), *The Edge of Words* (2014), *Meeting God in Paul* (2015), *On Augustine* (2016), *Being Disciples: Essentials of the Christian life* (2016), *God With Us: The meaning of the cross and resurrection—then and now* (2017), *Holy Living: The Christian Tradition for Today* (2017), *Christ the Heart of Creation* (2018), *Being Human: Bodies, Minds, Persons* (2018), *Luminaries: Twenty Lives that Illuminate the Christian Way* (2019), and *The Way of St Benedict* (2020).

Aside from such writings on a wide range of theological, historical, and political themes, he is a noted poet and translator of poetry, and, apart from Welsh, speaks or reads nine other languages, including Spanish, French, German, Russian, biblical Hebrew, Syriac, Latin, and both ancient (koine) and modern Greek. In 2013, he delivered the Gifford Lectures at the University of Edinburgh on "Making representations: religious faith and the habits of language". In 2016, his play, *Shakeshafte*, was staged for the first time. It concerns a meeting between William Shakespeare and Edmund Campion, a Jesuit priest and martyr. Dr Williams suspects that Shakespeare was Catholic, though not a regular churchgoer.

He was awarded the Oxford higher degree of Doctor of Divinity in 1989, and an honorary Doctor of Civil Law degree in 2005; Cambridge followed in 2006 with an honorary DD. He holds honorary doctorates from considerably more than a dozen other universities, from Durham University in England to Wycliffe College and Trinity College in the University of Toronto, Canada, and from the Katholieke Universiteit Leuven to the Evangelisch-Theologische Fakultät at the University of Bonn. He has successively been elected a Fellow of the British Academy (in 1990), the Royal Society of Literature (in 2003), and the Learned Society of Wales (in 2010).

Upon his translation to the see of Canterbury, he was sworn of the Privy Council, and, upon his retirement, Her Majesty the Queen bestowed the Royal Victorian Chain upon him. As if this were not honour enough, seven years later, in 2019, he was named as the third PM Glynn Lecturer on Religion, Law and Public Life.

Dr Michael Casey, director of the PM Glynn Institute, wrote in the preface to a pamphlet containing the lecture, "Lord Williams is one of the most distinguished religious leaders and public figures of our time, and the topic of his lecture goes directly to major questions at the intersection of religion, law, and public life today." Dr Casey explains that the lecturer "brings immense learning, a sensibility acutely attuned to the complexity of human habits and motivations, and deep reflection to the consideration of what we owe each other as human beings, and how we should disagree and live together if we are to have some sort of shared future." He particularly admires the way in which the lecture, "in putting down 'a serious caution against the idea of the *enlightened* state as universal arbiter of conviction,' invites us to consider what we can do to foster communities, institutions, and practices which enable us to learn from those with whom we disagree over matters of deepest conviction, to help build a durable life in common."

The third PM Glynn Lecture was entitled "Overcoming political tribalism", and it is reproduced at the beginning of this volume. The lecture commences with some reflections on the way the word 'tribal' has been used in modern or Enlightenment societies. Tribal attitudes or behaviours are aberrations from the norm. For a modern or Enlightened mind to classify another group as an aberration because it is irrational, and hence doomed, deviant, or outdated is, it is argued, itself to demonstrate a tribal mindset. In other words, for me, as a modern person, to label someone different as 'tribal' is for me to adopt a tribal mindset in relation to that person. The argument then develops in four stages.

First, it is argued that, in order to overcome a tribal mindset, I must engage in an activity of learning. Learning is a way of telling a story. It involves telling the story of change in a way that identifies some feature as salient to understanding the change properly. This is to acknowledge that what might once have seemed like an adequate way of doing something is no longer adequate. If we forget that learning occurs in this way, we are at risk of believing that we possess the complete, timelessly self-evident truth. This can lead us to a point at which we insist on the rightness of our stance, and our inability to remember that it is in fact the product of a story of learning may prevent us from appreciating that others might have another story of learning; that there is more to discover. Enlightenment thinking is particularly susceptible to this problem, and so it can lead to a form of tribalism that occurs when rational people cannot understand how other (strange) people might approach a problem in light of a different story of learning.

Secondly, overcoming political tribalism requires more than mere civility: it requires the creation of a shared language. This requires some investment in the 'stranger' and the stranger's way of approaching a problem. A shared language expands the possibility for mutual recognition. It will not necessarily lead to a shared view about a contentious issue, but it will allow us to capture in language the commitments of those with whom we disagree, and this allows us to see that our disagreement is not simply a contest for brute power.

Thirdly, there is an ethical need for a culture to have the capacity for such change. This involves learning. It requires us to be open to understanding the logic that motivates both sides of a disagreement. Enlightenment thinking can hinder this activity when it delegitimises ways of thinking about a problem that do not seem to be rational. This can lead to a form of Enlightenment tribalism, and we need to learn how to overcome this by paying attention to the ethical seriousness involved in other ways of approaching a problem.

Finally, it is suggested that there might be a special role for religious ideas of tradition and community in our efforts to overcome tribalism. Religious community can remind us that the most polarising political debates are usually not about absolute and final ends, but rather are about methods and processes that are simply means to shared ends. In an even more profound way, some religions remind us that although our learning involves what can be verbally and conceptually communicated, it never tells us the complete truth about "the inexhaustible agency from which life flows". So, religion urges us to be cautious about just how far we as individuals can get through the application of reason. Religion can become as tribal as anything else, but it also has the capacity to help move us beyond tribalism.

The lecture was established in 2017 with the intention to provide an eminent person with the opportunity to address an important question at the intersection of religion, the law, and public life. We were honoured to hear from one who reached the loftiest heights of the law, when J. D. Heydon QC delivered the inaugural lecture on "Religious 'toleration' in modern Australia: the tyranny of relativism". That lecture was published with eleven responses in *Today's Tyrants: Responding to Dyson Heydon.* We then heard, delivered from the heights of public life, Dr Jesse Norman MP's "The moral basis of a commercial society", which was published in *The Market's Morals: Responding to Jesse Norman*, together with a collection of twelve responses. This volume provides the opportunity to complete the triumvirate with a lecture by one who has soared to the highest places of public religion. His lecture is now published with a collection of twelve responses.

This collection of responses begins with three essays that reflect on Williams's theological and political perspectives. Nigel Zimmermann's essay attempts to locate the lecture in the broader context of Williams's theology and churchmanship. Amanda Stoker and Ben Etherington then locate the lecture in relation to modern and postmodern politics. Stoker argues that Williams overdoes the critique of Enlightenment or modern societies, and that the real problem lies in the pernicious influence of postmodernism. Etherington takes a rather different line, arguing that Williams gives Enlightenment or modern society rather too easy a ride, and that, in fact, modern politics (that Stoker defends) is more fundamentally flawed than Williams recognises.

Anthony Ekpo and Cristina Gomez then consider the relationship between Williams's thought and Catholic theology. Ekpo suggests that Pope Paul VI's concept of *novus habitus mentis* provides a foundational idea that is missing from Williams's account of shared language. Gomez, on the other hand, investigates the high degree of comity between Pope Francis's concepts of 'integral human development' and 'integral ecology' and Williams's approach to overcoming political tribalism.

There follow four essays dealing with challenges for overcoming political tribalism in a colonial world and a digital world. Kerry Pinkstone and Austin Wyatt reflect on residual problems of colonialism. In the Australian context, Pinkstone discusses the challenges of shared language, particularly in the context of constitutional recognition of Aboriginal and Torres Strait Islander peoples—unfinished business that is the legacy of attitudes prevalent in the colonial era and the Federation debates that shaped the Australian Constitution. Wyatt addresses the Western context more generally, and the way in which orientalism continues to encourage tribalist responses in the West to 'non-Western' peoples. Moving from the persisting legacy of a past era to the emerging problems of a new one, Ethan Westwood and Sandra Jones discuss challenges presented by the digital world to which the Internet gave rise. Westwood draws attention to the phenomenon of the filter bubble, and the way that this causes the digital space to increase, rather than overcome, political tribalism. Jones is interested in a narrower group: autistic people and the parents of children with autism, who have become tribalised in large measure through their digital interactions.

Finally, the collection ends with three essays, by Annette Pierdziwol, Michael Casey, and Scott Stephens, which speak to the lecture as a comment on the crisis that contemporary democratic politics currently faces, and the solution that Williams sees in learning to understand one another's political stances as reasonable—in their own way—and susceptible to compromise. Pierdziwol argues that Williams's cure for the crisis is only a partial cure, and that any sustainable solution will have to include an affective component identified by Martha Nussbaum: love. Casey sees the solution as lying in a form of friendship, rather than love. Stephens believes the missing component is citizens affirming their sense of shared purpose, which ought to underpin a politics committed to serving our life in common.

The lecture was delivered in the Peter Cosgrove Centre at Australian Catholic University's North Sydney Campus on 8 September 2019 in the presence of Sir Peter and Their Graces the Catholic and Anglican archbishops of Sydney and the Catholic Archbishop of Melbourne. To this august gathering was added the further ornament of the distinguished presence of Her Excellency the Governor of New South Wales, who has graciously consented to provide a foreword to this volume.

The Third PM Glynn Lecture on

Religion, Law and Public Life

Overcoming Political Tribalism

Rowan Williams

Perhaps we should begin by establishing one obvious point. The very word 'tribalism' tells a story, about the demeaning or marginalising of cultures that we call 'tribal': whether in Tsarist Russia or in British Imperial India, 'tribal peoples' were a category needing special administrative measures, on the assumption that they represented a departure from the norm of social life or citizenship. And to speak of 'tribalism' or of 'tribal' attitudes and behaviour is to mark out certain kinds of human behaviour as aberrations from the norm; these behaviours may be intriguing, even sympathetic in certain ways, but they are ultimately both doomed and deviant; they are forms of life that are, at best, noble but destined for extinction. And the rational and 'normal' dominant group will, where necessary, with whatever appropriate expressions of regret,[1] act as the agents of fate, and accelerate this extinction by one or another form of genocide. It may be unequivocal, literal extermination: the hunting and slaughtering of Indigenous peoples, in Australia and Tasmania; the slower extermination of the San peoples of Southern Africa or the original inhabitants of the Caribbean. Or it may be what is now widely recognised as cultural genocide: the 'native schools' of Canada saw it as their calling to 'kill the Indian in the child', to redeem children from the curse of their inherited identities and affiliations so as to make them proper citizens of the nation.[2] Genocide can wear the dress of benign progressivism as well as that of murderous violence.

The 'tribal' is that which is doomed because it has failed to change. In the prevailing mythology of modernity, what is normal is a particular kind of rationality which sees itself as universal—as opposed to the partial and unreasoning traditions that have been overthrown by enlightenment. What is unfamiliar or impenetrable to the rational mind is thus not just something *other*; it is something *past*. It does not belong *now*.[3] And—as we'll see shortly—this 'now' is a moment that is presented as timelessly and obviously true. The illegitimacy of non-'modern' social patterns, 'tribal' life in the most literal sense, lies in their belonging to another age. What modernity confronts and opposes is (naturally enough) the past; what is other to modernity is essentially *over*, and its persistence is an anomaly. What's more, it is—again, naturally enough—seen as imperfectly human, so that life lived within these terms is less than it should be, less than the fullness that we now enjoy and have grown into. Non-modern life is a *deprived* life, so that the efforts to eradicate it can be seen as part of a struggle for fullness of human experience—the struggle that shows we are, in the odd but persistent phrase, 'on the side of history'.

Of course, it is never quite so simple: the uncomfortable fact is that non-modern patterns of life have not gone away. We (rational moderns) are still *actually* contemporary with our supposedly displaced predecessors; and the recent history of massive and overt genocide in the twentieth century has left us uneasy about older methods of ironing out cultural difference. Apologies have been offered for the cruelties of colonial rule, and a new configuration of ideas about human rights has done something to balance out the crudities of sub-Darwinian models of cultural evolution. But the default setting of 'modern' society (Westernising, 'technocratic', rights-oriented, and committed to individual autonomy as an ideal) is still to picture itself as the rational norm for fully flourishing human existence. It does not really see itself as *a* culture among others. And this is why the record of modern (post-sixteenth century) European encounter with the 'tribal' other is illuminating in thinking about the much wider question of political tribalism. The fundamental irony lies in the way that the claim to *universal* validity made by modernity entails a sharply exclusionary rhetoric about what is not standard modern practice, even when the human rights culture of the day mandates some sort of tolerance for non-standard communities. As will become clear, the lack of a fully coherent philosophical anthropology in modernity has a lot to do with the tensions, conflicts, and imbalances that this leaves us with. But for our immediate purposes, the point is a simple one: modernity's rejection of an outmoded or superseded other is itself a 'tribal' response, to use the word in the pejorative sense that has become normal for Western society.

Of course, to identify modernity and the broadly 'Enlightenment' mindset as a form of tribalism is *not* to license some sort of easy relativism, nor is it to seek to reintroduce unchallengeable systems of traditional authority. It is simply to say that modernity becomes toxic at many levels when it loses the capacity for self-critique, and when it canonizes the myth of automatic improvement through time. 'Being on the side of history' is a wholly vacuous notion; and if we want to speak of and support something we can call a *progressive* political agenda, we need to be clear that we are assuming an anthropology with some normative force—i.e. that we are assuming there is actually an objectively 'better' place to arrive—not appealing to the naked process of change as such for moral (or indeed rational) justification. There are many diverse stories of social and intellectual change to be told; and when we tell these stories in terms of advance, triumph, liberation, or indeed enlightenment, we are telling them as stories of *learning*.

This is, I want to suggest, the key concept in any challenge to 'tribalism' in its malign sense. When we now speak about a tribalised politics, the politics of zero-sum conflict, and polarised interest groups, when we characterize these groups as sharing a set of moral priorities that may not be obviously connected with one another but are held by the same sort of people, and are considered in aggregate as constituting 'liberal' or 'traditional' identities, then we are creating a political discourse in which it is very hard to admit having *learned* anything. This is a bit paradoxical: we have seen that the superior claim of modernity is that it is the deposit and effect of change, where other forms of life have failed to change. But the truth is that change is not the same as learning or 'progress': learning is a way of *telling the story of change*, selecting this or that feature of what is remembered, making and testing links that are not instantly self-evident, identifying moments of significant conflict and the perception of choices to be made. Like all serious knowing, it is a *cultural* affair, bound up with inherited and internalised habits of seeing and representing, habits that have proved trustworthy or sustainable. When learning occurs, it is when sustainable habits encounter difficulty and frustration, and new habits and strategies emerge to modify what has been taken for granted. And when we tell such a story, we acknowledge that what *once* seemed adequate may be challenged; that moments of conflict and difficulty may be generative; that therefore our practices of knowing and understanding are about responding with tolerable success to what we don't control. If we lose sight of how this complex process of adjustment actually works, we are in trouble.

What happens when we forget how to tell our story in this

way? We come to resist any notion that what we take for granted as settled is not instantly self-evident, and we lose the sense that engagement with the alien and the unplanned is a potential source of insight and enrichment. It is as though a willingness to tell the story of learning brings an unwelcome vulnerability for us: if we admit we have had to learn through complex and protracted interactions, we admit that a story of self-evident advance, an inevitable, *unarguable* advance in truthfulness, will not work. Contingency creeps in: things didn't have to be like this, and so things do not *now* have to be like this. And if that's the case, then argument and discovery are not over. There is always work to do in establishing and defending the truth or rightness of a consensus. And to the extent that this suggests an unwelcome strenuousness about our social discourse, an acceptance of ongoing difficulty, there is likely to be a degree of unspoken pressure to minimise the scope of this narrative of protracted learning, and to maximise the area of what is taken to be obviously and timelessly true, simply *given* (if we are free enough and wise enough to open our eyes). Denying this 'given' and obvious quality in current convictions comes to be seen either as malign anti-humanism or as a mark of mental and spiritual enslavement.

The more a moral or social position is taken to be timelessly self-evident in this way, the more moral *reproach* is attached to any doubt or denial of it—and so the less room remains for any attempt at finding a common language for debate and shared reflection. This particular aspect of political discourse is currently one of the major challenges to the future of democracy. A political debate in which your opponent is not merely mistaken, unwise, or uninformed but malignant and/or subrational is one in which (say) the winner and the loser in an election have no stake in accommodating one another after the vote; and this slips readily into majoritarian tyranny—however close a vote may be in simple numerical terms.[4] As I've argued elsewhere,[5] a democratic majority establishes roughly what a majority of citizens can recognise as *lawful*, and what it requires of the minority is to abide by that recognition: a majority makes the rules and has a claim to be obeyed, in the terms in which elective democracy is set up. What it does not and cannot establish is what must be recognised as *true* or *good*; which is why working democracies make provision for liberty of conscience, without which no intelligible *debate* continues. And if no intelligible debate continues, the elective process itself becomes an empty sham, a contest purely about interest and power. It is a moot question how far down this road some modern democracies have actually travelled; but that is for another day.[6]

It's perhaps worth mentioning at this juncture another aspect of our current social and intellectual environment that is perhaps not strictly material to our main topic but throws some light on the implications of Enlightenment tribalism as a search for timeless, 'unlearned' truth. We are notoriously governed by algorithms, via the electronic monitoring of our patterns of behaviour—especially preference and choice; and we are fascinated (and intermittently panicked) by the capacities of artificial intelligence to solve problems more rapidly than human minds. We are still awed by the ability of computers to win at chess, let alone to predict patterns of consumption and even preferred points of view on various subjects. We are encouraged to have high expectations of the capacity of AI to diagnose medical conditions, given its ability to process a range of reported data far more speedily and comprehensibly than a human physician. But precisely this last point reveals a key problem, admirably discussed by a British doctor in a recent article.[7] The diagnosing doctor retains two critical advantages. She or he is likely to have—or have access to—information about the social, personal, and relational context of a patient in a way that allows an interpretation of reported symptoms more nuanced than could be offered by a mechanical process; and they are also—simply as routinely functioning human beings—likely to have learned skills of 'reading' the time of a voice or the gesture and movement of a body. The latter is the sort of *cultural* skill that depends on one's own self-awareness as a bodily subject. 'Information', as conceived in AI terms, is, in contrast, not something dependent upon this sort of learning, whatever may be said about the learning capacity of AI systems; and, as the article mentioned points out, any informational blind spot in what is introduced into an electronic system remains an *absolute* blind spot, not merely a deficient understanding.

But the fascination and the high expectation persist; as if the timeless, mathematically constructed binaries of the intelligence system represent some sort of ideal for knowledge and judgment. It is as though we are *eager* to be 'defeated' by mechanical means, so as to prove that the ultimate, unanswerable mode of knowing is indeed bodiless and timeless—not learned in any familiar sense of the word. The romance with AI, the 'charm' and attraction, in Wittgenstein's word,[8] of 'knowing' that we are at the mercy of bare cause and effect, actors in a script written by a force other than ourselves, is a telling reflection of how and why we choose our myths in modernity: our dependence and materiality are as much an embarrassment as ever they were for an ancient Neoplatonist or Manichaean.

What we call tribalism is, in its contemporary forms, a curious and ironic by-product of rationalism. It takes for granted that we don't need to rehearse the labour and negotiation, the difficulties, the false starts, by which moral and political perspectives are arrived at—because then we don't need to see the perspective of the other as (to borrow a turn of phrase from Gillian Rose) 'invested', developed as a way of responding to and managing certain sorts of difficulty that I/we can *recognise*.

Political tribalism is above all a shrinkage of the scope of mutual recognition: I resolve not to think of the other's view as sharing any of the moral anxieties or emotional tensions I experience. Someone who supports assisted dying will characterize the principled opponent as emotionally deaf to the force of unmanageable suffering. A committed pro-life advocate will characterize the physician performing an abortion as a murderer. Brexiteers and anti-Brexiteers alike describe their opponents as undermining democracy. The critic of Israeli government policy is an antisemite, and the critic of antisemitism is a dupe of Zionist conspiracy. The Green activist who argues against the fiction of limitless economic growth is blind to the pauperising of vulnerable workers.

To be clear: this is not a bland appeal for civility in political debate. That would too easily be reduced to an appeal not to be so emotionally invested in our beliefs, which is a futile recommendation. It is an appeal for some kind of work to grasp the history and structure of the 'investment' of the stranger. And for any such work to advance, there has to be an exercise in translating this investment on the part of the other into terms that resonate for me. This points in the direction of one of the central aspects in any discourse that looks beyond tribalism—the formation of as much of a *shared language* as possible. Shared languages certainly don't necessitate shared views; but they enable a more protracted engagement on issues, an engagement that does not instantly turn into the naked contest of power. It means the effort involved for the pro-life activist in seeing the defender or provider of abortion as driven by a *recognisable* compassion for women deprived of agency and dignity, not as a murderer; as it involves the pro-choice activist in recognising the opponent of abortion as seeking to defend the most radically vulnerable of human organisms, the unborn child, not as a single-minded misogynistic oppressor of women. It means the pro-Palestinian taking time to weigh the human cost of antisemitism over the centuries and to recognise a common story of displacement and insecurity—and again, it means the mirror-image for the passionate Zionist, called to recognise the reality of profound insecurity and disadvantage that their absolutism creates on their own doorstep. The point is in no way to relativise or weaken commitments or to accept an indefinite standoff. It is to try and discover what the 'grammar' of another's moral energy has in common with my own, *as the condition for intelligent action.* Damien Freeman's illuminating essay on getting inside the Indigenous perspective in Australia's debates over the public acknowledgement of Indigenous history and presence[9] provides a helpful take on this in noting that movement happens only when we see that debate is not necessarily about different solutions to a single, clearly defined problem, but about the factors that make us see problems differently. When those factors are articulated and explored, it is harder to see a conflict wholly in terms of absolute victory and defeat: to recognise a credible moral perspective in the programme of a successful majority allows a minority to see where argument can continue; to recognise that an unsuccessful minority holds views with at least some roots in common with those of the 'winners' is to find a rationale for accommodating that minority. And, crucially, this labour of recognition can also serve in helping to identify and conceptually isolate those conflicts that *are* beyond ordinary argument and negotiation, those *ultima ratio* questions where common language can't be found because some political interest is systematically and deliberately not recognising the claim of fellow human beings: totalitarian and genocidal systems are by definition those that embody this refusal, this drastic abandonment of any intelligible claim to legitimacy. But, for our present purpose, the important thing is to recognise that political tribalism, insofar as it inexorably moves towards de-legitimising the other in debate, is a fertile seedbed for totalitarianism.

If this is more than just an appeal for civility, it is also more than a plea for empathy.[10] Mere fellow-feeling does not specify any solution to serious conflicts of power and to the inevitabilities of loss or cost in the processes of negotiating a shared future. The intelligent recognition of the history of another's moral perspective and the deeper intelligent exploration of one's own history in the same mode should illuminate the fact that, in the actual world of moral decision-making, especially when it is being done in the public and political sphere, it is virtually impossible to find courses of action that are without cost—that is, without some sacrifice of an ideal level of doing equal justice to diverse claims. And this in turn might dispose us to see our decision-making as a matter of *clarifying* problems, identifying claims as clearly as possible, and looking for a *sustainable* way forward. One of the difficulties in a climate so much dominated by the discourse of rights is the temptation to cast our decision-making in terms of the simple binary alternative of whether we are or are not honouring or realising a clearly-defined and discrete 'right'; not doing so would simply constitute a legal tort, taking something unlawfully from its owner. I don't in the least share the skepticism about rights discourse that is popular among some of my theological colleagues, including some for whom I have great respect;[11] but I believe it is essential for an intelligent, compassionate, and (to use the word again) sustainable political democracy to focus more on manageable solutions to specific unjust situations rather than being paralysed by maximalist general demands. To take an example many Western societies will currently recognise, there are many specific injustices and disproportionate challenges and sufferings experienced by people who are gender-dysphoric or who have undergone reassignment treatment and surgery. The default 'conservative' position which declares the whole thing to be impossible, misguided, blasphemous, or whatever has generally not been troubled to attend to the particular narratives of these persons, and is inclined to read the phenomenon as necessarily bound up with a general campaign of relativism and revisionism about human nature. But some sorts of generalising language about transgender rights have not helped either, because they move attention away from finding sustainable solutions to particular challenges or inequities, and play into the hands of conservative polemicists.[12] The right that matters is the liberty to act within the shared life of a society without unjust restraint and to contribute a perspective of self-understanding to democratic argument and discernment—rather than a list of particular entitlements whose denial is a taking away of lawfully owned 'property'.

All this, and more, is entailed in the business of looking for elements of common language. We could express it slightly differently by saying that it has to do with the work of constructing a *culture* that is capable of containing disagreement and managing change in ways that do not violently disrupt the life of a society. In the present political climate in many 'developed' societies, there is heavy emphasis on prescriptive and protective legislation; and this is in significant measure a mark of cultural failure or dysfunction. Some citizens—usually with good reason—are persuaded that they cannot trust their society to respect and protect their interests. Legislation around all sorts of questions, from 'hate speech' to gender pay gaps, reflects an underlying anxiety that some groups are silenced, intimidated, or otherwise disadvantaged to a level where the informal workings of a culture seem unable to offer a positive adjustment in their favour. And the larger and more complex the social unit, the more such legislated guarantees seem unavoidable. The trouble is that the apparent simplicity and decisiveness of the legal guarantee can give us an alibi for the more protracted work of cultural change—which involves just the kind of attentive narrative exchanges that we have identified as building shared languages and avoiding zero-sum tribalism.

The labour of cultural change, then, is a matter of looking for or constructing contexts in which narrative sharing is possible, and different groups and interests can work together at what a manageable (sustainable) future might look like—acknowledging that such a future will *not* be simply the embodiment of one group's ideals. This labour assumes a *general* willingness to learn, both in the sense of learning to understand an alien perspective and in the sense of devising new pathways and strategies. It acknowledges, above all, the fact that the other is not going away. As our opening reflections noted, one of the most dangerous elements of what I've called Enlightenment tribalism is the tacit belief that history has an automatic moral, value-laden direction such that the pre-modern or non-modern have no real legitimacy; their survival is an unhappy accident, and their eradication (with or without active persecution) is something *destined.* But if this powerful myth is challenged, if we come to see Enlightenment rationalism as another set of learned perspectives rather than a timeless and self-evident system, then what defines itself as rational modernity cannot simply assume that all other narratives will necessarily vanish. The other is not only still here but has a legitimate claim to be here, as a culture that managed, endured, and made sense. The Canadian poet and philosopher Robert Bringhurst captures this (characteristically) with force and clarity:

> Other cultural models have worked, and some of them have worked for long stretches of time. Are any of them perfect? Hugely unlikely. Does the tradition of Enlightenment thinking have something to teach them? Very likely. Do they have things to teach it? Almost certainly they do.[13]

Bringhurst is writing in response to an egregious example of Enlightenment triumphalism from Steven Pinker.[14] But he is at pains to insist that what he is *not* doing is turning his back on "good science and sober humanism".[15] The humanism that matters is a humanism that reckons with the actual diversity of learning and conviction, and the science that matters is a science that knows what it can and cannot measure. The indispensable contribution of European Enlightenment is its challenge to any authority that refuses to explore and justify its perspectives; ironically, one of its great insights is the reminder that authorities have histories. The mistake is to see this as a simple demand of *any* form of inherited custom or belief because of the conviction that the act of critical exploration arises from a universal rationality that needs no justification. It is parallel to the question I have discussed elsewhere of the distinction between 'procedural' and 'programmatic' secularism in society—the difference between critical habit or practice (essential to any 'sober humanism') and the systematic de-legitimising of all habits and practices except those of a self-conscious instrumentalist version of intellectual modernity.

To sum up so far. Pushing back against political tribalism means recovering an awareness of what human learning is actually like as a time-taking, relationally shaped process, with a sense of purposiveness built into it, an inchoate and often elusive or unspoken conviction about what human meaning is at its fullest, that is more than just an intellectually dressed-up chronological snobbery and superstition. It means nourishing those practices and intuitions that allow space for hearing the memory of discovery and conviction that lies behind an opponent's view and seeking to recognise comparable kinds of moral energy. And it means accepting that the other, even the opponent, has a continuing presence and stake in a shared social territory, so that the task becomes one of finding what sustains that shared territory and defends us from zero-sum violence in our conflicts. In plainer terms, beyond political tribalism lie a deeper literacy about our histories, a commitment to identifying the grammar of a common language, and the work of negotiating a shared future by looking for solutions that have a degree of durability and credibility even if they are no-one's ideal.

In the final part of this lecture I want to turn briefly to some of the ways in which the practice and language of religious communities may turn out to be a key element in resisting the tribalism we have been thinking about. Lord Acton observed[16] that religious liberty was not just an *instance* of political liberty but its foundation: a state acknowledging freedom of religious belief and behaviour is acknowledging that it is not the sole measure of the identity of its citizens, and thus that a citizen may quite properly regard himself or herself as *answerable* to something more than the commands of a superior political power. From this acknowledgment, fully understood, flow a whole range of elements in what we now take for granted in democratic states, especially the rule of law and the rights of minorities. "Everything is politics, but politics is not everything", it has been said; or, to put it rather differently, the truly emancipated citizen is someone who is not *just* a citizen. Civic virtue is bound up with affiliations and convictions that have more than just civic roots and sanctions.

So a first respect in which the religious community is a resource against reductive polarisations in politics is the reminder it offers that purely 'political' debates are not routinely about issues of final and absolute import; they are typically debates about method and process, and the underlying debates about ends rather than means are never going to be decided by political means—that is, by the contingencies of who it is that happens to be exercising power. And this also means that resistance to the determinations of political power in the name of conviction or conscience cannot—except in the most extreme of circumstances, and not even then with clear legitimacy[17]—

be conducted by violence, by a counter-bid for coercive force. "Politics is not everything"; the most significant kinds of human solidarity do not derive from or depend on the state, and—as a range of nineteenth and twentieth-century Christian political thinkers have argued[18]—the apparatus of the state serves as a broker of interests between a natural diversity of local and voluntary networks of affiliation. Whatever 'orthodoxies' the state imposes need to be justified as intrinsic to its essential role of securing protection under law for all (which may also involve calling communities to account for their own failures in securing protection and human dignity, as in the realm of child protection).

But we can go further and look at the positive as well as the negative in the role of communities of belief. Religious discourse is heavily invested in narratives of learning; most notably the 'Abrahamic' traditions tell stories of unexpected developments, initiatives from beyond history, which clarify and reconfigure human goals—the law of Moses, the recital of the Qur'an, the creation of a new and unlimited form of solidarity and mutuality in the Church. To belong in the communities thus created is to be offered a variety of models of learning—and, in all the major traditions, to be reminded of the gap between what is verbally and conceptually communicated, or enacted in gesture, habit, and ritual, and the inexhaustible agency from which life flows. In the Christian tradition, this is the 'apophatic' style of theology, reminding us that *truthful* speech about the divine reality is not necessarily exhaustive, final, definitive speech. There is always more to see and more to learn, and the paradigm of faithful life is precisely 'discipleship', the status of a learner; the classics of spiritual practice set out the shape of a journey.

History and the acceptance of an always incomplete and developing understanding are central themes for most religious traditions: the very idea of 'tradition' (contrary to the conventional modern understanding of it as static and beyond argument) carries the assumption of a continuing process of acquiring skills of perception and judgment, and testing these skills in changing contexts.[19] The subject or agent in a religious context is a person in the process of formation within a community that teaches habits of seeing and responding and that urges caution about supposing we have access to final certainty simply as individuals equipped with tools of reasoning. Jan Zwicky, another noted Canadian thinker and writer, sums up the ways in which we might redefine classical, 'Socratic' virtues for our own day as comprising self-awareness (including awareness of our limitations), courage, self-control (the restraint of naked appetite), justice (a commitment to ordered harmony in relations and the freedom of each to contribute a particular gift and skill to the whole), 'contemplative practice' and compassion.[20] Her discussion of 'contemplative practice' is an exploration of some of the resources offered by traditions that train us in *attention* to what is before us, the silencing of an aggressive, fearful, greedy age. As she says,[21] this does not always accompany or arise from specific religious doctrine, but she is clear that the kind of ritual practice that slows and focuses our seeing of the world is a distinctive contribution from religious tradition, essential for the balanced wellbeing of person and community. And this slowed and focused attention is a habit that cannot survive in the neighbourhood of the sort of tribal allegiances that make my value or security dependent on knowing who my enemy is and where I must fortify my borders.

Attention is another word for the kind of unpressured listening to the narratives of neighbour and stranger that we considered earlier. As such, it is a key element in the search for a common language and a sustainable shared future. To be aware of the time it takes for me—as an ego normally inclined to fear or greed—to acquire the habit of seeing receptively or generously is to be aware potentially of the time in which another lives, and of the various pressures and contingencies that shape and perhaps abort or mis-shape—their learning. It is a specific against the idea of a truth that can be delivered instantly as a timelessly valid given. But of course, once this is said, it will very reasonably be pointed out that religious traditions are not exactly unfamiliar with claims to timelessly valid, instantly accessible truths; and worse still, with an identification of the disciplines of communal learning and acquired habit with obedience to a teaching 'caste', employing sanctions. The unhappy disjunction in some modern theological thought between 'teaching church' and 'learning church' is a dramatic illustration of the problem. Arguing for the vital necessity of tradition and the positive role of religious conviction in modern society is not credible if there is no *self-critical* energy in a tradition, and no living practice of contemplative formation.

Which is to admit, of course, that religion, theology, liturgical tradition, and so on can become yet another 'tribal' system of allegiances. There is, as we all know, polarisation within communities of faith between 'guardians of tradition' and 'revisionists'. To identify as a 'traditionalist' is to define an essentially political stance—and so, I would argue, to do much less than justice to tradition itself as a mode of prolonged learning and exposure to truth. The sad fact is that—as some have put it in recent discussions—tradition is an 'orphan' in the contemporary cultural climate; rather than being the unselfconscious transmission and reworking of an organic set of skills and habits, it becomes an option, preferred by certain individuals in the trenches of our culture wars. And if that happens, it is in danger of being reduced to an item in the market of ideas, to be defended against competitors.

Notoriously, one of the things we simply can't do is to construct a programme for being unselfconscious. As we noted earlier, part of the characteristic struggle of modernity arises from the effort to resolve by prescription what is better resolved by culture—a version of what Simone Weil famously identified as the root of most of our cultural problems, our refusal to "cure our faults by attention and not by will".[22] But this phraseology gives us, in fact, an important clue about where we look practically for strategies to subvert tribalism. We need to be asking what the communities, institutions, and practices are that allow a more comprehensive and 'attentive' social imagination to come to birth. The answer points to an almost chaotically wide spread of phenomena. Nurturing such an imagination includes the patient attention to stories and priorities not native to us that we were reflecting on a bit earlier; and this requires the construction of environments in which there is enough trust for such things to be articulated. This in turn regularly means finding common actions and purposes, so that we grasp that in some respects the other's 'investment' is like our own. It may be as simple as the sports team or the choir; it may be outcome-focused—a credit union or a school parents' association; it may be a community arts project, a development charity support group or a visiting rota at a residential care home. Or of course it may be a religious community—and evidence suggests a high level of local involvement by people with religious convictions in activities like those just listed. To discover or rediscover forms of human solidarity and exchange that do not depend on identifying enemies and are not so driven as to find no time for mutual listening is probably the most significant preservative for law-governed democracy in contemporary societies. It creates a context in which what we *owe* to one another is learned in the time it takes to build a durable level of trust.

This may seem to be some way from theories of modernity or tradition, but it puts some flesh on what lives look like 'beyond tribalism'. But the thesis of this lecture is not only about community organizing as a means of social salvation. It is also that the presence in complex and pluralist societies of certain groups holding themselves accountable to more than an immediate social consensus is something democratic societies should be glad of: it keeps fundamental argument alive, and obliges settled secular perspectives to articulate argument and justification for what they take for granted. It witnesses to what has been called the *longue durée* of our civilisation,[23] reminding modernity of how other and sometimes very alien cultures have managed their environment—including managing the environment in the most literal sense. Remember Robert Bringhurst's challenge as to what technocratic modernity has to learn from the 'pre-modern'—which takes us back to our starting-point in the destructive confrontation between 'enlightened' Western humanity and its ill-fated neighbours in the high days of colonial confidence.

And—to repeat the point—none of this is an appeal to reverse the Enlightenment challenge to arbitrary autocracy, or a bid to establish religious authorities as arbiters of law and ethics in plural and secularising societies, or a relativising of the achievement of experimental and theoretical science. It is to put down a serious caution against the idea of the 'enlightened' state as universal arbiter of conviction, simply because this risks binding any kind of public moral discernment to the power of a majority. The deepest problem with political tribalism, the all-or-nothing rhetoric of the electoral politics of the United States or the Brexit debates nearer home, is that it turns its back on the possibility of horizons expanding—even where fundamental orientations don't change radically. And conversely, the major challenge of moving beyond such tribalism, with its scapegoating and demonizing and lack of collective self-scrutiny, is the building of a culture that is confident, trustful enough to give time for perspectives to interact and interrogate one another and themselves. Building such a culture is intrinsic to building something more than a 'strong' state or nation—the creation of durable human solidarity, within and between states. And if communities of faith—unapologetic but reflective, critical and exploratory—are part of this as they should be and need to be, we may yet salvage an intelligent, compassionate, and pluralist democracy from the wreckage of so much contemporary political habit. From the point of view of one particular faith at least, this is a faint but not delusive shadow of the vision in Christian Scripture of the innumerable multitudes "from every tribe and tongue and people and nation", finally united in the loving recognition of one another because they all recognise the infinite act and gift to which finite human hearts and wills must respond.

Responding to Rowan Williams

1

THE REASONABLE POET AND THE CLAMOUR OF THE CROWD

NIGEL ZIMMERMANN

I have only met Rowan Williams twice, but on both occasions he left a deep impression. The first was on the eve of His Holiness Pope St John Paul II's funeral in 2005, for which the then Archbishop of Canterbury was speaking to a large gathering of Anglican clergy for the 150th anniversary of the Societas Sanctae Crucis (Society of the Holy Cross) in London.* His Grace was giving a lecture to mark the occasion, and then was scheduled to head directly to Heathrow Airport for a flight to Rome, and on the following day was to gather with other dignitaries for a significant and sad farewell to the 264th Bishop of Rome.

* The Society of the Holy Cross, also known by its Latin title, Societas Sanctae Crucis (SSC) was established by the Reverend Charles Lowder in 1855 as an Anglican Congregation of Priests who are bound together with a common rule of prayer: "To defend and strengthen the spiritual life of the clergy, to defend the faith of the Church, and to carry on and aid Mission work both at home and abroad" (from the SSC objects). A common objective of SSC clergy is the reunion of Christians together with the Holy See without dilution of Anglican identity and practices.

Archbishop Williams was not a member of the Societas Sanctae Crucis, and no doubt considered some of the theological positions of those clergy—'Catholic priests of the Anglican obedience'—rather conservative. Nevertheless, he was warmly welcomed as their honoured guest, and a spirit of charity filled the air as he spoke movingly of the sacrificial nature of the Eucharist and its deep importance to him in his Christian devotion.

My second encounter took place some years later at Australian Catholic University, when the University's public policy think-tank, the PM Glynn Institute, hosted Lord Williams of Oystermouth to present the annual PM Glynn lecture. As well as speaking to many hundreds of guests, Lord Williams kindly talked with about twenty of us over an informal lunch, gathered together in the Apostolic Delegation Room at ACU's North Sydney campus; the same room in which His Holiness Pope St Paul VI received the Catholic Bishops of Australia in 1970. Incidentally, it was Paul VI who graciously presented an episcopal ring to the 100th Archbishop of Canterbury, Michael Ramsey, in an emotional moment on 24 March 1966, telling a story of Christian unity more eloquent than any speech or letter.*

In my first encounter, I met Archbishop Williams wearing clerical black as a young, naïve Anglican clergyman; in my second, I was a Catholic layman, having 'crossed the Tiber' some ten years earlier. In that time, I had travelled my own theological and intellectual journey, but it was in the second encounter I felt rather closer to Lord Williams, in sympathy and in respect. This closeness is something worth exploring, because it took place

* The event is quite literally a tearful historical moment, because according to Archbishop Ramsey's private secretary, he spontaneously burst into tears when His Holiness placed the episcopal ring he had worn, as Archbishop of Milan, upon the Anglican Archbishop's own hand. As told by Fr John Andrew, the event signified a less than subtle recognition of mutuality in the episcopate, despite complex historical and theological divides: see Fr Andrew's account in the *National Catholic Reporter*, 17 October 2003.

in a context in which our broader Western culture has embarked upon the ways of tribalism ever more violently, a path for which Williams has been trying to provide correction. In this respect, regardless of your religious views, Rowan Williams lends a voice to reason over the panic-prone crowd, and a gentle re-assuring voice in opposition to the shrill abuse of the other that keeps rising, cloaked in the veneer of inclusivity and diversity.

Having established the peculiarly modernist context in which 'tribalism' has become a term of colonialist expansion, carrying within itself a post sixteenth-century anthropology of human progress and enlightenment, Williams shines light on one of its parents, that of rationalism. The rationalist perspective, when it proceeds in the direction of ideology, can too often become a normalising principle of totalitarianism, beginning with the manipulation of language. The practices of communication are immutably cultural, and always contextual even when they have a universalising aspect, and as such must be learned before and during their exercise. In other words, language opens up a vista of communicative possibilities among people. Perhaps those possibilities are endless, but they are not vacuous of concrete meaning or of forming a conclusion based on reasoned reflection and debate. In fact, this way of understanding language is a means of conceiving of our inherently human capacity to *learn*, and to keep learning with others.

To learn with others is not necessarily an instrument of power in any bare and simple way; if it is an authentic act of learning it must be mutual, as any wise lecturer knows, even when teaching undergraduate students on their first foray into university life. The teacher and the student must learn from one another, even if one speaks with a certain authority, however mediated. Learning is a way of being human, and when the ways of learning suffer, so too does any intelligible work of political activity, because we fall back into the ancient and oft-repeated act of annihilating strangeness or alterity. Williams refers to examples in contemporary discourse such as the treatment of Indigenous peoples, and their relationship with non-Indigenous peoples. During his visit to Australia in 2020, before travel became impossible due to Covid-19, Williams spent some significant moments sharing with Indigenous people, and he bore a gracious interest in their stories which would put many non-Indigenous Australians to shame. In this way, the act of learning is more artful than scientific, tending to a nuanced reading of texts and people that remains sensitive to cultural difference without resorting to the blandness of 'progressivism' and its allusions to universal meaning.

For Williams, religious discourse has a capacity to learn and to facilitate the learning-with-others that he suggests. While religion is not at all immune to the temptation to become totalising, it also has the happy distinction of having expertise in contemplation and community.[1] Perhaps taking Williams's thought further, a new revelation at this juncture in the story of the rise and fall of modernity might be in the very failure of Enlightenment ideologies to be self-critical—a sin towards which the Enlightenment philosophers accuse Christianity in the West of being particularly prone. Williams takes up Simone Weil's identification of the root of so many cultural problems as being found in the refusal to cure our faults by attention rather than by will. Religion, certainly in the Abrahamic traditions, is intensely expressed by attention and not by the will, which perhaps is why historically a certain democratic element can remain so vibrant in religious communities. That is to say, regardless of personal strengths, attributes, and circumstance, each member of living Abrahamic religious traditions has a certain freedom to attend to the object of worship and to the subject of faith; one's office or particular responsibilities in the community has little to no bearing upon one's capacity to have insight into, or accessibility towards, some knowledge and practice of the divine. For many Christians, this is epitomised in the mother of Jesus, Mary of Nazareth, who is considered higher than the angels and other saints, and yet she was not a member of the first group of Apostles who served Christ, nor a member of any formal leadership order in the early church.[2] That is to say, her high authority is because of her holiness and not by virtue of being a member of any hierarchy. Her love and fidelity to God was enough to make her first in the order of holiness, and this modelling of virtue is the guide for all other members of that religious community.

This brings me to a point that Williams makes so eloquently, but which can also raise new problems for us. The descriptions of tribalism that Williams utilises are evidently conscious of the dangers of a mob-like mentality in the new world of social media, virtue-signalling, and politics as a zero-sum game. He is prophetic when he says that the "deepest problem with political tribalism, the all-or-nothing rhetoric of the electoral politics of the United States or the Brexit debates nearer home, is that it turns its back on the possibility of horizons expanding—even where fundamental orientations don't change radically." When we fall into political tribalism, we do not just flatten the meaning of the other person, or others generally with whom we disagree, but we annihilate them in their significance. Moreover, we dismantle our own ability even to share a widening horizon of meaning with others. Our imagination is reduced and the chance of community, let alone something as beautifully evocative as communion or fellowship, is fashioned into a lie; a fabrication of what is possible. Williams here is at his most profound, unmasking the idols of a secular age with the long patient work of the reasonable poet, one who can see the best in every point of view, and who prompts us to avoid a superficial fragmentation into categories like left and right.

This is a poignant truth that Williams is uniquely well-disposed to articulate, given his heroic efforts at holding together the Anglican Communion during an epoch of theological division, broken communion, and moral disagreement. But it is perhaps exactly this genius of Williams that can be the most perplexing in an era of magnified subjectivity, in which there is no such thing as 'the' truth so much as 'my' truth, or even more fluidly, 'my reality'. To return to the point about Mary above, it is in this intersection between the particular and the universal ('my' truth and 'the' truth, so to say) that Williams's perspective becomes something that, at times, fails to 'land'. That is to say, as an ecclesial leader and as a poet and intellectual, he has prophetically cast clarity on the confused knots of meaning that contemporary life gets itself wound up within, but he will often hover just above the landing point of making the conclusive statement that his own logic suggests. In a remarkable and articulate homily before an ecumenical audience in 2008, Williams outlined some touch points of a way of seeing Mary that was inviting, inclusive, and pointedly devoid of disunity.[3] In his homily, he refers to the visionary of the Shrine of Our Lady of Lourdes, Saint Bernadette, as well as to Saint Teresa of Avila; he repeats the 'Jesus Prayer' of Eastern Orthodox piety before returning to C. S. Lewis in his own Anglican tradition; and finishes with reference to Elizabeth of the New Testament and the stirring of new life within. Williams draws on a rich and ecumenical tradition, and highlights common points of reference, but is reluctant to be too concrete in outlining the path ahead for separated brethren.

This is important because tribalism is not in any way a mere abstraction along the pathway of modernity (or its end, as the case may be), but now an integral reality in its wake. If you survey any debate in either online social media or in the news, you will find expressions of anger between political opponents which lack courtesy and reason, and which labels the other in increasingly crude terms. People are not in rational disagreement; they are embroiled in a heightened display of anger and mutual ridicule. Elements of this are not altogether new, but what is novel is the immediate technological facilitation of such mutual ridicule before a chorus of cheerers-on. The old image of the townsfolk being stirred up to rise with pitchforks as an angry mob no longer works. Rather, the angry mob is ready with the pitchforks at all times, tuned in and logged on to defame and belittle the enemy as soon as the bell is rung. We cannot say that the enemy is right or wrong, rather we paint them as either good or bad, a move that is both juvenile and de-humanising.

Such changes in our political discourse are the fruits of a deeper antagonism towards tradition and continuity, one we might call a cultural change. Like others in the past who have undergone historical cultural change, we are probably the least qualified people to evaluate critically what is happening and its long-term significance. Nevertheless, if we overlook it or take it at face value, we do a disservice to our own generation. Rowan Williams has referred to some of the changes we are undergoing with reference to a kind of "cultural bereavement".[4]

It is when he reflects on the precise problems through which our culture is passing that Williams is at his most eloquent. In *Lost Icons*, Williams covers a myriad of topics, from philosophical nihilism to Sigmund Freud to war to the genius of Jim Henson and The Muppets. In that book, I would draw attention particularly to what Williams writes about the topic of remorse, and especially after some reflections on the Holocaust. Williams picks up on insights from his friend, the writer Gillian Rose, and considers the problem of remorse for both individuals and whole communities with regard to the horrors of the Second World War. Rose had critiqued aspects of Holocaust Museum exhibits, and particularly photographic displays of those who lost their lives to the Nazis and those who survived. Williams picks up from Rose the need for self-critique, and a kind of non-compliance with the museum-centric approach to discovering the stories of the Holocaust. In becoming vulnerable before the strangeness of the other, we turn against what Williams elsewhere has described as political tribalism with its proneness to mutualising strength against a common enemy, and to better understanding ourselves in relation to other people. That is to say, to return to a theme we began with, to the art of learning *with* others. To enter into an authentic sense of common and social instruction, a setting in which we are all students learning to become friends, is also to be remorseful of what has gone before. As Williams puts it:

> Rediscovering remorse, then, has a lot to do with the capacity of a culture to leave room for the non-heroic, to celebrate the vulnerable and even the comic. It may sound very strange to associate the sense of the real otherness of a lost object or of another's suffering with the dimension of the comic: but comedy is one very important vehicle for acknowledging and dramatizing human involvement in a world that is very imperfectly controlled by human planning, and in which the wills and desires of others frustrate the tyrannies of any single human ego.[5]

And perhaps this is the insight that strikes us so perplexingly in the language Williams draws from so many different traditions—that I am not a lone ego exercising power through my own will or channelling it through the violence of the tribe. I am a human *subject*, and I am working alongside *other* human subjects, equally vulnerable to the temptations and trivialities of others in the midst of serious cultural upheaval.

In the end, we will need to 'land' our thoughts more concretely than where the poetic Williams leads us. But that aside, his persistence in the ways of reason and beauty show a pathway in which political tribalism can be overcome. For Rowan Williams, tribalism in its contemporary guise is inherently unreasonable and, ultimately, has no compass for what might be truly beautiful, and so no matter how rational it may seem to some of its adherents, it can never escape the echo of its own self-defeating mantras. The trouble of course is that those joining the chants of the tribe in full flight have already narrowed their vision to simply what the crowd wishes them to see, and so they reduce the other through acts of violent discourse that lends itself to the ways of blood and fury. Overcoming such a discourse is not achievable by setting up camp as a 'revisionist' or a 'traditionalist', at least not in the political markers that Williams is worried about, but more along the lines described by Simone Weil, referred to respectfully by Williams in his PM Glynn Lecture. For Weil, the political walls we build between ourselves and our neighbours are the very constructs the most holy of men and women have seen fit to destroy. In the witness of 'saints', we see how the particularities of one life apply themselves for the universal vision of all others:

> It is true that we have to love our neighbour, but, in the example that Christ gave as an illustration of this commandment, the neighbour is a being of whom nothing is known, lying naked, bleeding, and unconscious on the road. It is a question of completely anonymous, and for that reason, completely universal love.[6]

By such measures are political excesses, and the tribalism that cultivates them, overcome.

2

Overcoming Intellectual Fragility

Amanda Stoker

It is not difficult to agree with Rowan Williams's assertion that our society is currently affected by a kind of political tribalism that allows one tribe to consider an opponent, with a different perspectives on an issue, as "not merely mistaken, unwise, or uninformed but malignant and/or sub-rational". It is similarly not difficult to agree with his view that there needs to be a willingness among strangers to slow down, listen to one another sincerely and with genuine attention. It is indeed part of the way we go about learning and showing empathy to one another. But it would be a mistake to think that the causes of political tribalism are just an exaggerated belief in the primacy of Enlightenment thought, a bias for modernity, and a dismissiveness of non-Western cultures.

That is to oversimplify his argument, of course, for Williams's point, I take it, is that a subtler form of tribalism arises. It is no longer that we form tribes based on our ancestry or the colour of our skin. Rather, we form tribes based on how we think, and have developed a practice of believing those who do not think like us are being irrational. By my reading, he urges us to consider that even when, as individuals, we are trying to think rationally, we don't always see the complete picture. Accordingly, we should try to open our minds to different thinking rather than dismissing the 'other' as irrational.

None of this is wrong. The real question, though, is: why have we adopted this practice of being tribal in the more subtle sense?

It means we should consider how we arrived here. For it seems that in the space of only a decade or two we have gone from being neighbourly and tolerant of differences in political view, to intolerant, comfortable only with those who inhabit the same political 'bubble'. This is borne out by data from the United States that shows a sharp rise in the physical siloing of populations of people of similar political views and families that cannot tolerate political differences.[1]

Part of the problem is our hyper-busy lifestyle. The ability to listen slowly and carefully to our differently-minded neighbour is difficult when the two-working-parent household is overscheduled, financially over-stretched, and consequently frazzled. The quick sound bite fits our schedule. Improving that can be approached from two angles: either finding ways to lower the cost of living—necessitating the confrontation of uncomfortable questions about our approach to energy production and labour-market reform, for example—or revisiting the material aspects of our values and how we live them. Our parents or grandparents' generation (depending on the age of the reader), were generally content with a home with one bathroom, shared bedrooms, and no media room. They could afford to have one parent stay home—or perhaps the invention of machines that make domestic duties more manageable has opened up choices that weren't there before. The frenetic pace we keep is, in many ways, the product of our choice to avail ourselves of as much of the material world as we can possibly afford. It is almost certainly more than we need.

Another part of it is the digital transformation of the last two decades, and the way that it has shortened our attention span. The media delivers a twenty-four-hour news cycle—which offers only a shallow glimpse into complex issues rather than exploring shades of grey—because that is what consumers demand. It is cognitive too—research on the impact of smart phones and tablets, for instance, on the developing brain show that they are not conducive to the development of deep thinking, sustained attention, or appreciation of that which doesn't flash like a poker machine.[2]

Rowan Williams notes that those who are enthusiastic about Enlightenment thinking are also guilty of tribalism. I'm sure that at times that is true of all human beings, and that it is, to an extent, part of human nature. Williams is right to observe that no one—even those who are enthusiastic about modernity—is necessarily immune. Yet, I would suggest that the decline in enthusiasm *for* aspects of Enlightenment thinking and teaching are part of the reason for the rise of the modern form of tribalism. Perhaps that is where the distinction lies: between the pre-modern tribalism with which Williams's essay opens, and the problematic behaviours of our time which make up this modern and more subtle form of tribalism. There is some irony in the observation that while Enlightenment thinkers might be dismissive of the pre-modern tribal society, Enlightenment thinking offers what is, in my view, the path *out* of modern tribalism.

Our education system no longer teaches logic or rhetoric unless it is carefully sought out at one of the few Australian universities that bother to teach it today. That's a problem, because without an appreciation of the value of logical reasoning, it is difficult to move beyond the emotive response—to consider the evidence, ponder contrary perspectives, and perhaps admit to having learned and even changed one's mind. Without an understanding of the art of rhetoric, even our best logical thinkers can't communicate their ideas to people who would benefit from that understanding. Indeed, in most areas of life and work now—especially politics—to admit of having learned and changed one's mind is treated as a sign of failure rather than strength. Demonstrations of such vulnerability are treated as an invitation to slaughter rather than a sign of growth.[3] That is a pity.

The harm caused by the absence of logic from our primary and secondary education systems, and its rarity in the tertiary sector, exacerbates another cause of tribalism: the primacy of emotional guidance for decision-making that is fashionable as both a parenting and educational trend. This trend is the subject of a chapter in the 2018 book, *The Coddling of the American Mind: How Good Intentions and Bad Ideas Are Setting Up a Generation for Failure*, by American lawyer Greg Lukianoff and social psychologist Jonathan Haidt, an outstanding work that seeks to understand and explain the shift on American college campuses to remove from curricula and libraries ideas that might cause students discomfort or offence. It is the movement that sees demands for historical monuments to be torn down because of disagreement with some point of view or action of the person or people involved, and for speakers to be banned from campuses for the same reason. Lukianoff and Haidt observe that the object of universities is no longer to confront and challenge the thinking of students, but to protect them from words or ideas that might—even accidentally—cause that discomfort. It has caused definitional concerns: one person's 'intellectual challenge' is another's 'psychological harm', and in a litigious era, university administrations are always going to err on the side of caution. Lukianoff and Haidt trace the oversensitivity of students today to overinvolved parenting styles in which 'helicopter'* parents do

* A style of child rearing in which an overprotective mother or father discourages a child's independence by being too involved in the child's life: in typical helicopter parenting, a mother or father swoops in at any sign of challenge or discomfort.

too much for their children, fuss over their academic advancement, safety, and schedule, and deny them vital opportunities to truly problem-solve, negotiate social conflicts, and experience the horror of the occasional scraped knee. They are perpetually told the world was dangerous, and that they need protection from it, from each other, and from themselves.

Lukianoff and Haidt call this approach to parenting, which involves protecting a child so much that it has the effect of causing real harm to the child's capacity to cope with life, 'vindictive protectiveness'. In the educational context, it manifests this way:[4]

> What are the effects of this new protectiveness on the students themselves? Does it benefit the people it is supposed to help? What exactly are students learning when they spend four years or more in a community that polices unintentional slights, places warning labels on works of classic literature, and in many other ways conveys the sense that words can be forms of violence that require strict control by campus authorities, who are expected to act as both protectors and prosecutors?
>
> There's a saying common in education circles: Don't teach students what to think; teach them how to think. The idea goes back at least as far as Socrates. Today, what we call the Socratic method is a way of teaching that fosters critical thinking, in part by encouraging students to question their own unexamined beliefs, as well as the received wisdom of those around them. Such questioning sometimes leads to discomfort, and even to anger, on the way to understanding.
>
> But vindictive protectiveness teaches students to think in a very different way. It prepares them poorly for professional life, which often demands intellectual engagement with people and ideas one might find uncongenial or wrong. The harm may be more immediate, too. A campus culture devoted to policing speech and punishing speakers is likely to engender patterns of thought that are surprisingly similar to those long identified

> by cognitive behavioural therapists as causes of depression and anxiety. The new protectiveness may be teaching students to think pathologically.

We should not kid ourselves with the notion that the situation is much different in Australia. There has been little work done to determine the extent to which the epidemic of poor mental health in Australian young people—about which we hear so much—can be explained, or at least be better understood, if viewed through the lens of this American research.

Our universities are remarkably homogenous environments—a situation that persists with some irony given there is no shortage of diversity policies that generally cover every attribute *but* intellectual diversity. They produce teachers for our next generation of pre-school, school, and university students. Those teachers have been exposed to little but the notion that ideas different to their own are harmful.

And then they teach our children that words you don't like to hear are violence.

My eldest daughter, who is six, recently argued passionately with me when I told her the old saying that "sticks and stones may break my bones, but words can never hurt me". She insisted that her teachers had taught her that nasty words were a form of harm equivalent to physical violence (though not in those words), and that I must be mistaken. The class had been taught it many times. Only now that we have talked about it at length does she see references to the old saying everywhere from music to books—albeit the older ones. She was wide-eyed with amazement when she first heard the phrase in a song; she had been so sure I had just made it up.

So much of this protection is well-meaning. There is an abundance of programmes teaching anti-bullying, and no doubt much of it is a response to the real and far too common examples of young people committing suicide in response to taunting by cruel peers. It is tragic, and the response to such tragedy is understandable. But there is also something to be said for the notion that humans are 'anti-fragile', to use Lukianoff and Haidt's terminology. Hardship metered out in sensible doses as we navigate the course of life enables us to become resilient. When we are cocooned from modest hardship, we either do not develop or we lose the resilience to cope with even ever diminishingly-sized life challenges.

The apparent rise in mental illness is not merely a matter of better awareness of its seriousness (although that is part of the story), or more eyes looking out for it in the health system. If it were simply a response to hardship, then rates would have been far higher in times of depression, recession, and war than they are now. They are not. Indeed, there is a correlation between high incidences of mental illnesses and lives of wealth and comfort.

Where does all of this leave us? With mentally and intellectually fragile people, quick to censor and deem perspectives other than their own as not just erroneous but harmful, violent, even criminal. And, when someone labels you harm-causing, violent, or criminal for your perspective, it's no wonder that the social fabric ruptures into tribalism. If those who think differently to you are not just good people with another view, or who are mistaken, or still learning, but perpetrators of an '–ism'; people with a '-phobia'—fundamentally evil—it is pretty harmful to the prospects of civil disagreement.

I suggest the escalation in modern political tribalism that sparked Williams's lecture is in large part the product of postmodernism and identity politics. There is a connection between the rise of the postmodern school—by whatever name it is referred to: intersectionality, cultural Marxism, gender theory, anti-colonialism, critical theory, identity politics, and the like—and the rise of tribalism. In its search for a power agenda in everything, postmodern ideologies badge every human relationship as one between victim and oppressor. Their solution is to identify victims of past injustice (often in past generations rather than in the present time) and elevate them over others, who, because of their oppressor status, are supposed to accept present punishment for the misdeeds of their predecessors.

This is toxic on many levels. The 'victim' develops a sense of entitlement to elevated status, and if it is not given, whether by government or others, it confirms victimhood. It is deeply disempowering to the victims, who come to believe they are not capable of transcending their minority status.

It also breeds resentment in those who are unjustly branded oppressors, whether based on the actual misdeeds of their ancestors or history rewritten ungenerously. And it makes our society tribal: adhering to allegiances to groups based on skin colour, sexuality, or gender.

And let's face it: we live in one of the most mobile societies in the world. Australia is one of the few places globally where it can truly be said that any person, however poor they may begin, who works hard and stays away from vice is near guaranteed to be middle-class by their life's end. In that context, the confected victimhood of postmodernism is self-indulgent.

Postmodernism uses physical attributes over which we have no control to justify our division into tribes of victims and oppressors. It leverages the story of victimhood over any ideas or history that might be contributed by the 'oppressor' side. It uses that victimhood to justify restraints upon free speech that today are greater than we have ever seen before in this nation. The lack of free speech, of intellectual diversity, and intellectual freedom feeds the mental fragility of our time.

The confinement of speech operates socially as well as legally.

Not only can you be dragged before a tribunal for expressing a perspective that confronts the worldview of a protected minority class; but you can also expect to be hauled before the human resources department for being insufficiently careful to avoid 'microaggressions' at work. You can be attacked by the enthusiasts of the victim tribe for insufficient sensitivity on social media or the subject of a complaint to university administration for 'triggering' a fellow student with an argument that confronts their perception of reality. It is truly absurd.

As societies like ours have writhed in our efforts to be sufficiently contrite to those victims, to smooth the path for their swift advancement and to ensure their 'identity' is not offended by ideas different from their own, a new elite has been formed. The criteria for entry is victimhood. If one's genetic attributes do not qualify for that status, sufficient endorsement of the primacy of the victim at all times will deliver a consistent second place.

The effect, though, is to silence people whose views don't align with the new elite. Most sensible people just don't need the hassle—or indeed the cost—of the fight with human resources, the courts, or with the tribunals. They don't want the social awkwardness or the risk of shame that comes with this kind of confrontation. It's easier just to put your head down and mind your own business. The effect, though, is to create the impression that the postmodern agenda is wholly accepted, and to deepen the well of silence.

It does not dispel the gut instinct in many people that something is deeply wrong. A generation ago, Martin Luther King Jr's famous words,[5] "I have a dream that my four little children will one day live in a nation where they will not be judged by the colour of their skin but by the content of their character" were uncontroversial. Today, many universities' policies indicate that to express a similar sentiment is a microaggression against people who are not Caucasian—presumably unless you are a 'person of colour'. Try and make sense of that one. The same applies for other 'protected attributes' under discrimination law.

What has always been the strength of Australian society has been that, as John Howard so aptly put it, "The things that unite Australians are infinitely more important and enduring than the things that divide us."[6] But the way identity politics seeks to separate and dehumanise different tribes within our society threatens our social cohesion. Taken to its extreme, it has the potential to descend into violence, of the kind that has become civil war in other nations.

From where do these concepts spring?

The international instruments we now call human rights law were put together at the end of the Second World War. It's impossible to think about those without recognising the impact that the two world wars themselves and the ideological circumstances of the time had upon the global psyche. The horror of the persecution of the Jews was fresh in the mind. The clash between Nazi fascism and Soviet communism was acute. The concept of rights that had evolved up to this point emerged from the natural rights tradition, with its roots in Judeo-Christian thinking. At their heart, natural rights are about the moral autonomy of the individual, and states are formed only to maintain those general rights. Rather than specifying what a person is entitled to, natural rights stand against anything that encroaches upon them.

But human rights law is different. It's specific, itemised, and purports to be exhaustive. Instead of setting out core general principles, it lists out everything the drafters regard as worthy causes, conflating negative and positive rights. Put another way, human rights law jumbles together protection for the individual against state action with demands that the state take particular action. There's a world of difference between the protection of an individual's right to pursue his or her own goals without the interference of the state (so long as you aren't bugging anyone else), and a demand, for example, that the state tax other people to provide you with particular services.

The 1948 Universal Declaration of Human Rights stated unequivocally that everyone has the right to freedom of opinion and expression—but it didn't impose any obligations on states. It wasn't a treaty as such, just a declaration. Dissatisfaction with the lack of obligation in the Universal Declaration led to the International Covenant on Civil and Political Rights.

It was adopted in 1966, and in article 19 included an apparently bold right to freedom of expression. However, article 19 was undermined by caveats permitting restrictions to "respect the rights or reputation of others", for "the protection of national security and public order", and the protection of "public health or morals". The last of those is particularly broad.

Article 20 laid the foundation for a new class of censorship. "Any advocacy of national, racial or religious hatred that constitutes incitement to discrimination, hostility or violence shall be prohibited by law." Incitement to violence had always been a limit on speech under the common law (and quite appropriately, no matter the circumstances), but it was never contingent on having "national, racial or religious" hatred at its core.

Incitement to discrimination or hostility had no precedent and no foundation until that point.

At first glance, this might appear a reasonable evolution given the horror of the Second World War. But article 20 had a political object that needs to be understood in its historical context. It reflected the clash of two worldviews that were competing for dominance: that of the West, with its belief in individual rights and liberties, and that of the Communist bloc, which absolutely did not.

In the negotiations for the ICCPR, the Communist bloc opposed freedom of speech being included. They did not believe people who held beliefs with which they disagreed should have a right to express themselves. They repeatedly attempted to insert a provision that said freedom of speech and the press should not be used for propagating fascism, aggression, or hatred between nations. That might not seem so controversial if you think of fascism as Nazism—but their definition of fascism included liberal capitalist speech. It became apparent in the debates that to the Communist bloc, fascism meant anything that was not Communist. It revealed that there was a desire on the Communist side to include sufficient exceptions as to facilitate whatever restrictions dictators wished to impose upon expression, in a way that would have rendered the more fulsome articles of the ICCPR null and void.

During the drafting of the International Convention for the Elimination of Racial Discrimination in 1966, the West agreed to "declare an offence punishable by law all dissemination of ideas based on racial superiority or hatred, incitement to racial discrimination"—either because they lost the debate or because they did not truly understand the provision's implications.

You cannot overestimate the size of this cultural shift. Now, instead of ensuring liberty, states were responsible for the *elimination* of intolerance and discrimination, something which *could not be achieved without* suppressing freedom of speech.

Let's not allow the Soviets to get away with their hypocrisy here. At the time, their constitution enshrined the right to freedom of expression and a free press—which would have been cause for laughter if so many people were not suffering, and 2,200,000 people were in the Gulag. The increasing emphasis on criminalising words that wound, offend, or hurt is the brainchild of the very barbaric totalitarian states with which Western states were battling in the Cold War. Soviet advocacy for restrictions on hate speech and discrimination were a play for human rights law to approve the suppression of dissent. We should not now be surprised that this has been their effect.

None of this is to endorse hate speech, discrimination, or even bad manners. But it is to say that we should not uncritically laud the impact of international human rights law in the way that so many undergraduates (and indeed politicians) do. It *is* to acknowledge the role that the proscription of particular ideas from the realm of healthy speech has in the tribalisation of our society. By deeming some words to be violence, we do not develop the strength to cope with words that affront us. It makes for an ever-lowering bar of tolerance for thoughts which are not our own.

Yes, we have become more tribal. Rowan Williams is, in my respectful view, right to say the answer must involve expanding our horizons, and that this involves "the building of a culture that is confident, trustful enough to give time for perspectives to interact and interrogate one another and themselves". But I would suggest he diagnoses one relatively minor factor of many, and in doing so misses much of the picture. I suggest natural rights, rather than international human rights; enlightenment education, rather than postmodern dogma; and intellectual freedom over vindictive protectiveness, are the way forward.

3

Tribalism as Anti-Politics

Ben Etherington

Rowan Williams takes a counter-intuitive line on the contemporary discussion of 'political tribalism'. The term has generally been used to refer to the phenomenon by which those in professedly liberal multicultural societies are turning their backs on a shared plural and secular space and embracing residual group identities, whether these be religious, ethno-nationalist, racial, gender-normative, or ideological. Contributing factors that are routinely cited include the social upheavals caused by the acceleration of capitalist globalisation, the 'bubble' effect of social media, spiralling inequality, and the demise of a centrist liberal consensus.

Williams proposes that a root cause, perhaps even *the* root cause, of tribalism in contemporary politics is an absolutism that was already baked into 'enlightened' secular modernity. The status quo that many regard to be under threat is, for Williams, itself a world created by the tribe of an "'enlightened' state" that casts itself as the "universal arbiter of conviction". For, where the laws and procedures of the secular state are regarded as an end in themselves, the battle for political power becomes a zero-sum affair: if your group wins power, your group's representatives rightly can dictate what's what. This gives Williams the grounds for the quite audacious claim that political tribalism is, in fact, "a curious and ironic by-product of rationalism".

To support this, Williams reminds us that this rationalist Western tribe has an imperial history marked by genocidal violence and that it continues to deny legitimacy to those social groups it casts as 'other'. Indeed, the pejorative connotations attaching to the word 'tribal' are themselves a symptom of a social order that fails to recognise that its institutions and norms have an anthropology and a history. The redress Williams recommends is a culturally chunky and dialectical liberalism. The variously constituted groups that make up our "complex and pluralist societies" should not rely on political procedures, defaulting to rights-based claims when they fail. We all need to undertake "the labour of recognition" required to negotiate real and meaningful differences. In one of the lecture's most resonant phrases, Williams calls on each of us "to try and discover what the 'grammar' of another's moral energy has in common with my own, *as the condition for intelligent action*". The dialectical energy of continual learning and mutual adaptation cannot be led by politics and the state. It is to be fostered in civil society—communities of faith, principally, but also other community-based organizations.

In some respects, this is a timely argument. In the face of new dogmatisms, it helps to be reminded of that which was dogmatic in the liberal triumphalism that so recently put itself forward as the best and only possible reality. Williams is encouraging us to develop a more robust and substantial liberalism, one that eschews the vapid teleology of capitalist progress. It is also helpful to have contemporary tribalism cast in the *longue durée* of the modernity in which it is enmeshed. What this broader historical perspective lacks, however, is the capacity to pinpoint why tribalism is rife at this particular moment. Perhaps this is intended: if we view the present as fluctuations on a seismograph of social crises that stretches back hundreds of years, we might forestall alarmism and attune ourselves to longer term solutions.

In other respects, Williams's argument feels like the right message at the wrong time. The good substantive liberalism that he advocates perhaps was needed most when, following the collapse of the Eastern Bloc, the bad proceduralist liberalism he critiques was unleashed. That was also the point at which an unthinking conviction about the capacity of markets to manage every aspect of human affairs gripped the world. We are now suffering the consequences of that misplaced confidence and, in my view, contemporary 'tribalism' reflects the struggles over the kind of society (or societies) that will emerge from these upheavals. In spite of his best intentions, then, Williams risks lapsing into an optimistic proceduralism at the moment when people are crying out for real alternatives to a global political economy that cannot solve the problems it has created. (This is evident in rather abstract formulations like "nourishing those practices and intuitions that allow space for hearing the memory of discovery" and "the building of a culture" that allows "for perspectives to interact and interrogate one another and themselves".) When we also factor in the cataclysmic implications of a rapidly warming ecosystem, the call for listening, learning, and accommodation might only play into the hands of those willing to use ruthless tactics.

I agree with Williams that the alternative social ends that we might seek—a collective flourishing in which "human meaning" may be lived "at is fullest"—cannot be derived from political activity alone. I am particularly taken by his notion that the labour of recognition undertaken between groups whose worldviews and/or interests are not readily aligned can help "to identify and conceptually isolate those conflicts that are beyond ordinary argument and negotiation". There are, without any doubt, roles for non-political organizations and groups in shaping our sense of what a good society ought to be and how we work towards it. But it needs to be acknowledged that the political behaviours that get labelled 'tribal' have arisen not from a surfeit of hands-on political involvement but a loss of political literacy and organizational participation. When one looks at the tactics employed respectively by Narendra Modi and Donald Trump to exclude Muslims from India and Mexicans from the United States, or those used by Boris Johnson to achieve Brexit, we see not the deployment of political persuasion but the mobilisation of hypostatised and residual ethno-cultural identities to achieve political ends.

All this leads me to wonder whether the problem that we are talking about is really *political* tribalism. As the political economist Elizabeth Humphrys has argued in the Australian context, such manoeuvres have succeeded where *anti*-political sentiment has prevailed.[1] Humphrys is referring to a phenomenon whose chief symptoms are declining trust in politicians, declining membership of political parties, and a declining share of the vote for major parties. Operating within hollowed out parties, those without scruples leverage the 'tribalistic' sentiments of their 'base' to gain power. Often this has meant those acting in the interests of a powerful minority are willing to throw the red meat of prejudice to the people who suffer the effects of their rule in order to gain their support. The common shorthand for this is, of course, 'populism'. A more conceptually precise way of thinking about it is as a practice of *hegemony*; that is, the means by which political consent is solicited through non-coercive means.

Writing during the period of Mussolini's rise, the Italian Marxist Antonio Gramsci turned to the concept of hegemony to spotlight the role of civil society in creating the conditions for consent among those in capitalist society whom the system of exchange and profit appeared systematically to be short-changing. For Gramsci, this principally meant the workers robbed of the value of their labour by the owners of capital. It was not simply that workers were 'duped' by the ideological messages of politicians. It was that they were active participants in complex networks of institutions and cultural affiliation that cumulatively served to reconcile them to life without effective economic or political power.

We might say that Williams is proposing a Gramscian solution: if tribalism has been cynically engineered in the sphere of politics, it will be for everyday people to work actively through local involvements and organizations to turn the tide. It will also allow them mutually to affirm their respective affiliations and commitments rather than a pragmatic need for "immediate social consensus". What this leaves out, though, is the question of the relationship between politics and civil society. Williams talks persuasively about learning but he does not broach the question of formal education—the space where the coercive power of the state and cultural work of civil society are fused. For some, most conspicuously the French philosopher Louis Althusser the separation between politics and civil society is itself an illusion of the hegemonic state. But one needn't sign up to his notion of the 'ideological state apparatus' to see that a lot of goodwill and hard work in civil society can quickly be usurped or folded back into 'tribal' interests. In 2018, the Australian Government allocated \$50 million to the celebration of the 250th anniversary of Captain Cook's voyage to Australia in the same budget that cut over \$80 million from the independent public broadcaster. There was no clamour for recognition of Cook. The ABC is, by far, the nation's most trusted media organisation. We need to keep in mind all the ways in which the realms of politics and civil society interact to create a hegemony that can stymy mutual recognition and foster hatred. When such a social logic takes hold, the urgent questions become: How can effective counter-hegemonic activities be stimulated? How quickly must their effects be felt before hegemonic forces are able fundamentally to change our sense of social norms? I leave these questions open. My purpose in this response has been to ask whether we need to reframe the problem as a matter of overcoming *anti*-political tribalism. We need *more* political activity and organizing just as we need more involvement in civil society. We need less passive consumption of politics and culture. This will take time and it will require intellectuals to get involved in the craft of politics and culture, not only to pronounce on them.

To conclude, I want to come back to the terms 'tribal' and 'tribalism'. Williams opens his essay with a compelling account of the way in which those who feel themselves securely to belong to secular modernity tend to disavow that which is tribal about this belonging. The denial that Western society is but "a culture among others" leads to "the systematic de-legitimising of all habits and practices except those of a self-conscious instrumentalist version of intellectual modernity". An acute point, it nevertheless leaves open the question of why *this* culture—the 'liberal West'—should be the one that disavows its 'tribal' nature while regularly succumbing to bouts of tribalism. All societies, including supposedly tribal ones, presumably create an atmosphere of relatively unselfconscious normative belonging. Other societies can act cruelly and imperialistically. Presumably, all require some kind of self-critical or at least self-correcting mechanism to deal with malign forces that arise within them. This suggests that the kind of modernity in which we find ourselves has a distinctively corrosive effect on our capacity to form functional and sustainable collectives. Applying ourselves to the labour of recognition and identifying conflicts that deny the possibility of recognition are a good way of testing whether we can achieve some kind of social sustainability in these conditions. But we may also be forced to confront, once again, the endemic failures of a society organized according to the logic of commodity exchange and be prepared to look seriously at radically different alternatives.

4

Are shared languages enough?

Anthony Ekpo

The ancient Greek philosopher, Aristotle, refers to the human being as a political animal (*zoon politikon*) and a social creature with the power of speech and moral reasoning.[1] In the Catholic tradition, politics is seen as "a high form of charity": an inestimable service of dedication for the achievement of the common good.[2] The common good is "the whole of those conditions of social life with which men and women, families, and associations can attain their perfection with great fullness and facility".[3] Politics is not meant to be "the slave of individual ambitions, of arrogance of factions or interest groups".[4]

In this day and age, however, politics has become a perpetual tribal war between the bold and the beautiful, the fast and the furious, where the end justifies almost any means. Cast your eyes across diverse nations and you will realise that in each of these countries there are similar patterns: political tribalism, inspired by a mentality of us-versus-them, political deadlock, and public frustration with the democratic status quo. There are arguments from different quarters, some condemning and others endorsing political tribalism. Some commentators believe that tribalism has been an inherent part of human history and that the human brain is wired to be tribal.[5] The British political theorist and social scientist, Alan Finlayson, argues that political tribalism should not be discouraged or shutdown, since politics and policy affect our lives directly.[6] According to him, "rather than put our tribes aside, we must be more and better committed to them. It is only by defending the interests we all share that we can protect our own".[7]

On the other hand, Amy Chua and Jed Rubenfeld, an American couple known for their expertise in law and ethnic conflict, condemn tribalism, arguing that it creates a mentality that does not see those on the opposite side of the political paddock as fellow citizens with differing views, "but as enemies to be vanquished".[8] As well, the governing constitution of a country in this climate is seen "not as an aspirational statement of shared principles and a bulwark against tribalism, but as a cudgel with which to attack those enemies".[9] Chua and Rubenfeld call for constitutional patriotism: "We have to remain united by and through the Constitution, regardless of our ideological disagreements." In his recently published book, *Vexed: Ethics beyond Political Tribes*, British author and journalist, James Mumford offers some explanation with regard to certain tribalistic behaviours:

> Tribes have their own heroes, saints, villains, stories, scriptures, symbols and colours. They are sites of intense emotional attachment. They confer meaning as well as secure survival. They have distinct takes on the past and visions of the future which characterized them. There are limits to the degree of internal deviance that can be tolerated.[10]

For Mumford, to defeat tribalism, there must be in everyone the "willingness to question package deals". He says: "refusing to have the parameters of our thinking, the range of options open to us, circumscribed by ideology may itself help us to move closer towards a profoundly different political environment".[11] The American political philosopher, Stephen Carter, proposes what he called an "etiquette of Democracy": an atmosphere in which people can engage in civil discourse in a respectful manner.[12]

In communion with those who condemn political tribalism, Rowan Williams, in his PM Glynn Lecture, speaks against political tribalism and proposes solutions to it. He argues that political tribalism, especially in its contemporary forms, is "a curious and ironic by-product of rationalism", marked ultimately by "a shrinkage of the scope of mutual recognition". For him, what is needed in politics is not just a conducive environment where people can engage in civil dialogues inspired by mutual respect—as important as this truly is—but also, and more importantly, the forging of "shared languages".

According to Williams, shared languages can be formed where there is "some kind of work to grasp the history and structure of the 'investment' of the stranger" and where efforts are invested in discovering and understanding "what the 'grammar' of another's moral energy has in common with my own". Shared languages are not necessarily "shared views", "but they enable a more protracted engagement with issues, an engagement that does not instantly turn into the naked contest of power". Williams argues that appeal for shared languages is not "a bland appeal for civility in political debate". For him, it is more than mere appeal to civility or empathy, as these cannot "specify any solution to serious conflicts of power and to the inevitabilities of loss or cost in the processes of negotiating a shared future".[13]

While Williams's argument would appear to be valid, it seems to be a second step in the continuum of eradicating political tribalism. The first step is working to develop what, in Catholic theological circles, is often expressed with the Latin phrase, *novus habitus mentis* ("a new way of thinking"). The phrase, *novus habitus mentis*, was first used by Pope Paul VI.[14] This Latin expression can be translated literally as "a new habit of the mind" or "a mind with a new disposition"; as well, it can be translated as "a new mentality" or "a new mind".[15] Having seen the tensions that occurred between different factions at the Second Vatican Council, which took place from 1962 to 1965, Paul VI called for a change in mindset, especially in the revision of the Church's law, which was meant to reflect all that was advanced at the Council.

Novus habitus mentis is the willingness to enter into "a new field of vision" or a "new horizon".[16] It is the disposition to listen with fresh ears and a receptive heart. This is not a matter of simple deduction or induction; rather, it is "a matter of courage and determination to accept the uncertainty that the new environment brings. To face such a new field of vision which is partly known, partly unknown, is an act of the whole human person: feelings, perceptions, understanding, moral sense of values, all play their part."[17] A new mindset is the disposition and willingness to explore the world out there that may be completely foreign to our preconceived ideas. This disposition helps us to become full, conscious, and active participants in what Williams calls "the labour of cultural change" on the road to developing shared languages.

Indeed, genuine shared languages would be impossible without a change of mindset. The development of a new way of thinking gives birth to the conversion of our political imagination and to the emergence of new meanings, that is, shared languages. The internal disposition of the one engaged in the work of forging genuine shared languages is of decisive and indispensable relevance. The closest that Williams comes to this first step occurs when he uses the phrase "general willingness" while talking about the labour of constructing contexts in which narrative sharing is possible. He says: "this labour assumes a *general willingness* to learn, both in the sense of learning to understand an alien perspective and in the sense of devising new pathways and strategies". One would have expected him to offer more reflection on this "general willingness", since it is an important epistemological and hermeneutical moment in the continuum of forging shared languages, in view of eradicating political tribalism.

Let us imagine forming shared languages to be like 'singing from the same hymn sheet', that is, an arrival at a creative symphony from a paralysing cacophony that is usually instigated by discordant voices. This presumes the collective disposition and understanding of the need to turn every cacophony into symphony, and singing in a mutually agreed language or playing in a mutually agreed key is a way of achieving this. First of all, there must be the disposition and willingness—a mutual new way of thinking—to turn the discordant and cacophonous into the symphonic, hence, the need to sing from the same hymn sheet.

In 1953, the maverick Anglo-Austrian philosopher, Ludwig Wittgenstein, coined the phrase "language games", and used it to refer to the shared conceptual and linguistic parameters that make human interaction possible. Wittgenstein argues that language possesses its own unity and order, just as a game of cricket or soccer does, because, like a game, language is a consensus of shared human activity.[18] For Wittgenstein, while language is by its very nature shared, it ultimately remains a game, where words acquire meaning by their use. Put simply, for Wittgenstein, every language is a shared language, and every shared language is a language game. The danger in applying Wittgenstein's understanding of shared languages to political debates is that it can become a game, which can be twisted and manipulated. Everything is fine when everyone plays by the rules within the broad framework of shared languages.

Although Williams uses the expression "shared languages", it is not clear that he intends these shared languages to be understood in terms of Wittgenstein's language games. It would appear that he intends this expression to mean the effort to resist the temptation of allowing the parameters of our thinking, the range of options open to us, to be circumscribed by ideology. In other words, he is advocating for an expansion and fusion of horizons in political debate, in difference to political tribalism born of antagonistic relativism. While it would not be fair to argue that Williams's "shared languages" is a clarion call for a neo-Wittgensteinian language game, I believe that it runs the risk of becoming a language game that can be manipulated.

Williams's "shared languages", in all its simplicity and depth, can become a game or a metaphor for some "regularity and order in 'getting along' or understanding what is being done with words, symbols and sentences" in political debates.[19] *Novus habitus mentis*—that collective new mindset and disposition—is therefore needed to prevent this from happening. It guarantees a genuine conversion and expansion of political horizons, marked by an honest effort to see with the eye of the *other* and to identify and analyse the factors that make us see problems differently.[20] In order to arrive at genuine shared languages devoid of manipulation, a new mindset is needed as a first step.

Reflecting on ways in which religious practice and language can be a key element in the task of resisting political tribalism through the formation of shared languages, Williams makes reference to the idea of "discipleship" in the Christian tradition. In this context, a disciple is one who has the understanding that "there is always more to see and more to learn". A disciple views life primarily as a pilgrimage and each of us as a *viator*, a pilgrim travelling along the way. The status of a disciple is that of a learner who is on a journey of discovering the mystery of God, which can never be "exhaustive, final, definitive"; for in revealing himself, God also conceals himself. A good disciple acquires the habit of seeing receptively or generously and, in Williams's words, listening attentively to "stories and priorities not native to him".

This quality of a disciple is an attribute of one with a new mindset, it does not see the *other* as an unintelligible and ignorant enemy to be destroyed. A new attitude of the mind is seen in the realisation that one does not know it all and that one's particular political viewpoint is not a "universal gospel" that should be shared by everyone. With this disposition, everyone arrives at the political table, not with the tribalistic "I see what you see but I see more" mentality, but rather with a new attitude of "tell me what you see and I will share what I see, and perhaps together, we can see more into the future in the task of working for the common good". This new disposition paves the way for the forging of genuine shared languages and guarantees their growth. In short, the formation of genuine shared languages, immune from language games, would be impossible without a new disposition, a new attitude of the mind.

5

Overcoming Tribalist Colonialism

Cristina Lledo Gomez

We are in an era of the so-called 'postcolonial' age. But as postcolonial scholars tell us, we are far from living in a society without a trace of colonialism.[1] In truth, colonialism* exists and persists, insidiously and in largely uncritical ways, in our laws, systems, structures, ways of being and interacting. The hold of colonialism is as such that there are many descendants of colonised peoples who have lost identities, creating identities for themselves by believing that the only real way to get ahead in this world is to become 'white'; literally, as in making one's own skin lighter in colour, and metaphorically, that

* Colonialism, as used in this essay, is the thinking and practices used by colonisers upon first peoples, to promote their culture as the norm, by any means, including bullying, domination, oppression, and denial of the equal dignity of first peoples and their descendants, as non-'white' persons (the act of colonisation). Colonialism has lasting impacts including its effects on the mindsets of people who have been subjected to it and their descendants. Postcolonialism, as explored in this essay, involves in part a colonised mindset which develops after the colonial era has formally ended and yet the impact remains. Tribalism is consequently understood in this chapter as referring to people who do not necessarily live in collectivist societies but adopt a tribal mindset. This approach of applying a tribalist mindset in a non-collective society will be discussed further in the essay.

is, adapting to the culture of their Western colonisers, including the negative aspects, of individualism, consumerism, domination, and bullying, and seeking endless exponential growth. This desire to be 'white' physically and in one's own way of thinking and interacting is evidence of colonial mentality and it is a form of internalised oppression.[2] Other characteristics of colonial mentality are: "denigration of the self; denigration of the culture or body; discriminating against less [Westernised] in-group members; and tolerating historical and contemporary oppression."[3] In general, colonial mentality can be viewed as "a broad multidimensional construct that refers to personal feelings or beliefs of ethnic or cultural inferiority."[4]

Filipinos are an interesting case study of a colonised people since their country was invaded three times: first by the Spaniards (1565-1898), then by the Americans (1898-1946), and briefly by the Japanese (1942-1945) before America (1945-1946) regained power until the Philippines gained its national independence on 4 July 1946. The reinforcement of inferiority through multiple colonisations is undeniable. In her recent book, *Racism and Resistance among the Filipino Diaspora*, sociologist and urban ethnographer Kristine Aquino argues that Filipinos master the language of their colonisers in order to "position themselves closer to colonial power".[5] But this act by the Philippine diaspora alongside the act of "distancing [themselves] from loud and crass Filipinos who speak Tagalog or English loudly in public spaces or from embarrassing Filipinos who speak imperfect English with a Filipino accent"[6] appear as signs of colonial mentality.

As a Philippine-born Australian migrant, I am particularly interested in the effects of colonisation upon the Filipino diaspora. There are few research pieces which explore the experience of Australian Filipinos and none as yet which focus upon their psychological state as a result of being a colonised people. But there is research which does show the psychological effects of colonisation upon Filipino migrants to the United States of America. One recently published article shows they experienced high rates of depression, suicide, and eating disorders, among other mental health issues, due to colonial mentality.[7] This is connected to the inability to foster a positive ethnic identity development, especially when one is on the very land of one's own coloniser.[8] This shows colonialism is well and truly alive, even among descendants of the colonised, in this so-called postcolonial age.

It is with much relief and gratitude then that I read the beginnings of Rowan Williams's lecture, which critiques the use of the word 'tribalism' and points to its denigrative association towards indigenous peoples, the colonised, and those who live a supposedly "inferior" way of life compared to Western "rational modern" standards. Williams challenges this narrow mindset which argues that rationality and modernity are the superior and only valid ways of existing and living today and also challenges the idea that 'tribalism' is something bygone and irrelevant. He reminds his audience that "non-modern tribes" are here to stay (despite their significantly diminished numbers as a result of colonialism) and if anything, contemporary Western society has more to learn from them than ever before.

I note the irony of the use of the word 'tribalism' to describe and to challenge political groupings/affiliations. In reality, one often finds in Western culture that individual interest takes priority over a group's interest. The individual aligns himself or herself to a group only insofar as the group serves self-interest. Once group identities become challenging or difficult for an individual, ties are readily broken with the group. There is no sense of membership or loyalty to them for it was never about the tribe, it was always about the individual and his or her vested interest.

In contrast, an indigenous sense of tribalism can be quite different. The indigenous culture is largely a collectivist culture and therefore takes seriously the group's concerns, rather than focussing exclusively on the individual's concerns. Sometimes this can be excessive and unbalanced and consequently detrimental to the individual. But when the group authentically seeks the good of all of its members, even in their differences, individual ties are then not so easily unbound because of disagreement or highly incompatible ideas and conflicting personalities.

I do not wish to present a romantic or homogenous picture of indigenous peoples or collectivist societies. Sometimes, some indigenous groups do exemplify the 'tribalism' caricature at its worst. This was recently evidenced in a report showing Papua New Guinean tribes at war with each other for the last three years, until they signed a peace agreement facilitated by a group of locals.[9] Whilst the caricature exists, it is unfair to apply this picture to all indigenous cultures or collective societies. It is an inappropriate and unhelpful image for Australia, a nation that aspires to a greater commitment to improving Indigenous peoples' lives, self-concept, and the possibility of their constitutional recognition.

Another way of looking at this is to assume that individualist societies would have non-tribal mindsets and inversely, traditional and/or collectivist societies would have tribal mindsets. Yet, as we know of our Enlightenment/modern societies, they are individualist rather than collectivist and they seem to harbour people with tribalist mindsets (oppositional approaches)—hence the need for Lord Williams's speech. Inversely, traditional societies expected to have tribalist mentalities do not have such mindsets but if they gave up their collectivist tendencies and retained tribalist mentalities, then that is doubly unfortunate for that society. The challenge then for traditional peoples as they enter the modern world is to retain their collectivist approach to community whilst letting go of any sense of a tribalist mindset. Likewise, Enlightenment/modern societies must grapple with tribalist mindsets as individualist societies, possibly turning to the wisdom and experience of collectivist societies.

As a Catholic theologian who has a particular focus on issues of ecology and justice for the marginalised of our world today, including women, migrants, and indigenous peoples, I find Pope Francis's promotion of the Catholic social principles, 'integral human development' and 'integral ecology' via the 'synodal' way, as being paths that open up new possibilities for a fractured society. The very existence of the phrase 'political tribalism' in the Western context evidences this fractured existence. The beauty of integral human development and integral ecology is that they not only reassign those on the margins to the centre of concern (practising another Catholic social principle, 'the preferential option for the poor'), but, moreover, seeks to bring together people of completely different backgrounds and even completely opposing ideas by pointing to their interconnectedness, interdependence, and unity in diversity—which leads them to be open to each other because they must find a way to be together in this one world despite, and also because of, their differences. It is with these perspectives in mind that I read Rowan Williams's lecture, finding much resonance between his suggestions for overcoming political 'tribalism' and integral human development, integral ecology, and synodality. This essay will thus focus on exploring these resonances and how they may be of mutual benefit, exemplifying then the act of dialogue, which ultimately the two religious leaders, Lord Williams and Pope Francis, wish to impart as a way forward in an increasingly divided (Western) society.

Integral human development is not a new phrase for the Catholic world. Pope Paul VI was the first to use it in 1967, in his encyclical, *On the Progress of Peoples*.[10] But Pope Francis gave new life and great emphasis to integral human development by creating a new Vatican Dicastery in 2016 under its name.[11] Integral human development is best summarised in Pope Benedict

XVI's encyclical letter of 2009, *On Integral Human Development in Charity and in Truth.* 12 In this letter, Benedict explains that the church is not just concerned with simply praying or engaging in charitable acts. Instead, these actions are a means towards the promotion of something bigger: an anthropology, a vision of integral human development. Integral human development not only addresses the spiritual aspect of persons. It is also concerned with the development of the other dimensions of being human including the intellectual, emotional, social, financial, political, sexual, and psychological dimensions of a person. This development is also more than just about the individual. It is also about the development of the one human family in its diversity. Integral human development's great challenge to all persons is that even if one has a completely opposing perspective to another, both must find a way forward together, to exist in the same space, while respecting each other's differences or particularities. It is about more than merely tolerating the other.

The idea of integral human development finds helpful points of engagement with Williams's lecture on at least two fronts. First, Williams's proposition that "the lack of a fully coherent philosophical anthropology in modernity has a lot to do with the tensions, conflicts, and imbalances that this leaves us with." Secondly, Williams's repeated claim (at least twice) that "political tribalism is above all a shrinkage of the scope of mutual recognition" and that the formation of a shared language aims to achieve the opposite of that shrinkage of mutual recognition.

Integral human development works within the framework of Catholic philosophical anthropology. Its coherent vision of humanity includes envisioning human beings as a reflection of the God of goodness, capable then of goodness themselves, alongside their freedom to reject the goodness for which they were created. This informs their way forward beyond and through human tensions, inequities and conflicts. In fact, because of this anthropological vision, tensions, inequities and conflicts are seen as constitutive of human living and its complexities. Therefore, finding a way forward with the 'other' amidst, despite, and/or because of human tensions, inequities, and conflicts is seen as the only way forward if one is to find peace in the current chaos and into the future.

On the necessity of mutual recognition to overcome political 'tribalism', Williams proposes "the formation of a shared language", a "common language for debate and shared reflection" achieved through "learning" from one another about one another—to such an extent that one is prepared to "grasp the history and structure of the 'investment' of the stranger". Williams says "this is not a bland appeal for civility in political debate". It is rather a "more protracted engagement on issues . . . that does not instantly turn into the naked contest of power". Like integral human development, Williams proposes on one level the general call to an openness to the Other, going beyond toleration, even when differences are present. The difference between the idea of integral human development and Williams's suggestions here is that integral human development remains at the broad conceptual level, whereas Williams actually enfleshes this broad conceptualisation enabling a person then to arrive at the concept through graduated steps in thinking.

These points of engagement show the usefulness of Williams's thinking in helping to make concrete the broad concepts proposed by integral human development. The same dynamic will be found below as we explore the points of connection between 'integral ecology' and Williams's challenges to overcoming political 'tribalism'.

In my view, integral ecology incorporates integral human development. Whilst it is important to highlight the distinctive contribution of integral human development in the church's thinking, that is, that it is concerned with the whole person and not just his or her spiritual dimension, the idea of coming together for the common good, even when the other has opposing ideas to oneself, can be subsumed into the concept of integral ecology.

For Francis, integral ecology is about being able to "integrate and promote" all the inhabitants of a community or nation, "enabling them to enjoy 'good living'"[13] or *buen vivir*, as imagined in the Beatitudes.[14] The Synod of Bishops for the Special Assembly for the Pan Amazon region further explains, the concept of integral ecology:

> It is a matter of living in harmony with oneself, with nature, with human beings and with the Supreme Being, since there is intercommunication throughout the cosmos; here there are neither exclusions nor those who exclude, and here a full life for all can be projected. Such an understanding of life is characterized by the interconnection and harmony of relationships between water, territory and nature, community life and culture, God and various spiritual forces. For them, 'good living' means understanding the centrality of the transcendent relational character of human beings and of creation, and implies 'good acting'. This integral approach is expressed in their own way of organizing that starts from the family and the community, and embraces a responsible use of all the goods of creation. Indigenous peoples aspire to better living conditions, especially in health and education. They want to enjoy sustainable development that they themselves choose and shape and that stays in harmony with their traditional ways of life, in a dialogue between their ancestral wisdom and technology and the new ones acquired.[15]

The idea of living in harmony with others has many resonances with the indigenous Filipino concept of *pakikisama.* Literally it means 'trying' (*pakiki*) to be 'together' (*sama*). It can be interpreted as 'trying together' to 'be together' or simply 'trying to be together'.

The notion of *pakikisama* is so strong that, culturally, Filipinos are generally unable to say 'no' to an invitation. (Thus, when they intend to decline the invitation they say 'maybe' and leave the possibility of saying yes in the future to the invitation.) For it does not seem right to reject another person's efforts to connect with them. The idea of disconnecting, or cutting connection with another person is culturally unimaginable.

Whilst Francis created the Dicastery for Integral Human Development four years ago, showing his commitment to this concept, he has written more on the idea of integral ecology than on integral human development. Francis especially calls for a turn from an unhealthy inward-looking anthropocentricism to a vision that sees humankind in connection with all of creation, locating humanity not above or at the centre of creation, but just as one among many of God's interconnected creations. It is an extended vision of integral human development which encourages 'trying together' to be 'together' in the same space.

Francis dedicates two documents to integral ecology: *Laudato Si* and *Querida Amazonia.*[16] These documents contain many points of connection with Williams's key points for overcoming political 'tribalism'. Interestingly, both Williams and Francis converge on the concept of 'learning' as *key* to addressing either political 'tribalism' or ecological disintegration. Furthermore, they both promote the same desired outcome from learning, that is, a change or a transformation towards something new and lifegiving, not just for the self but also for others.

Williams says of learning:

> This is, I want to suggest, the key concept in any challenge to 'tribalism' in its malign sense . . . When learning occurs, it is when sustainable habits encounter difficulty and frustration, and new habits and strategies emerge to modify what has been taken for granted."

Similarly, Francis writes of education:

> The best ecology always has an educational dimension that can encourage the development of new habits in individuals and groups . . . A sound and sustainable ecology, one capable of bringing about change, will not develop unless people are changed, unless they are encouraged to opt for another style of life, one less greedy and more serene, more respectful and less anxious, more fraternal.[17]

Combining the insights of Williams and Francis: "The ways of learning or education involve listening" (Francis),[18] "grasp[ing] the history and structure of the 'investment' of the stranger" (Williams); "a communicative culture that favours dialogue, the culture of encounter" (Francis);[19] engaging "with the alien and the unplanned" even to the point of "unwelcome strenuousness" or "an acceptance of ongoing difficulty". For it is about "constructing a culture that is capable of containing disagreement and managing change in ways that do not violently disrupt the life of a society" (Williams); and finally, a call to unlearning, learning, and relearning "in order to overcome any tendency toward colonising models that have caused harm in the past" (Francis).[20] It is about "looking for or constructing contexts in which narrative sharing is possible and different groups and interests can work together" for "the other is not going away" and they have "a legitimate claim to be here, as a culture that managed, endured, and made sense" (Williams).

As per the dialogue between the concepts of integral human development and Williams's challenges for overcoming political 'tribalism' above, Francis provides a broader concept of integral ecology which can benefit much from Williams's more graded steps towards this broad vision. Inversely, Francis's vision of integral ecology serves to support Williams's specific suggestions as to how individuals can help to overcome political tribalism in their society. Both integral human development and integral ecology are concepts that can have meaning in the non-Christian and even non-religious contexts. But synodality is a specifically ecclesial term which I briefly highlight here simply to evidence that it is part of the Catholic imagination and even central to how that imagination envisions a way of being and interacting which is about connection and walking with the other, again even when the other is different to oneself. This is explained well by the Synod of Bishops for the Special Assembly of the Pan Amazon region in *The Amazon—The Final Document*, the document which foregrounded Francis's *Querida Amazonia* alongside other deliberations from the gathering of bishops in the Amazon in 2019:

> 'Synod' is an ancient word venerated by Tradition; it indicates the path or way that the members of God's people pursue together; it refers to the Lord Jesus, who presents himself as "the way and the truth and the life" (John 14:6), and to the fact that Christians were called "the followers of the way of the Lord" (Acts 9:2); to be synodal is together to follow "the way of the Lord" (Acts 18:25). Synodality is the way of being of the early Church (cf. Acts 15) and it must be ours. "As a body is one though it has many parts, and all the parts of the body, though many, are one body, so also Christ" (1 Corinthians 12:12). Synodality also characterizes the Church of the Second Vatican Council, understood as the People of God in their equality and common dignity with regard to the diversity of ministries, charisms and services. "Synodality is the specific *modus vivendi et operandi* of the Church, the People of God, which reveals and gives substance to her being as communion when all her members journey together, gather in assembly and take an active part in her evangelising mission" that is to say, in "the involvement and participation of the whole People of God in the life and mission of the Church".[21]

'Synod' itself derives from the Greek roots of *syn* and *hodos*, meaning 'with/together' and 'way/road'. Its literal meaning is thus to journey together. The whole Christian life is imagined as walking on a road of faith, a journey which one takes as a pilgrim on earth. For the church, the reality of God is revealed in Jesus, who walked with others without judgement, and who, through dialogue and discernment, opened them to growth and transformation. Journeying together with an openness to new possibilities is at the heart of synodality.

Synodality, integral ecology, and integral human development are concerned with more than just a philosophical concept of walking with each other in difference. At the heart of all three concepts is the trinitarian God who can exist only as a community, and particularly as a community of love and connection, even in their difference (Father, Son and Spirit). When one is called to walk with others, to connect, to understand unity in diversity, to entertain openness, dialogue, learning, unlearning, relearning, vulnerability, change, and transformation—one is called to reflect the trinitarian God and the dynamic of the Community of Three Persons. The call then to synodality, integral ecological conversion, and integral human development is ultimately the call to reflect the God of love who exists only in love, in connection—in the Christian view, this is the true reality of humanity and I suspect Rowan Williams's "overcoming political tribalism" is, at its foundations, about reflecting this trinitarian God who only exists in connection, in faith, hope, and love. Engaging with Williams's lecture as a Catholic theologian through the lenses of integral human development, integral ecological, and synodality has evidenced to me Williams's incredible gifts as author, public theologian, and pastoral minister. While often in Christianity one finds beautiful visions and broader concepts or ideals and leaves the 'fleshing-out' of the steps towards the ideals to its audiences, Williams has the gift of taking that audience (particularly the Western audience who prize rationality and reason) step by step towards the broader vision.* It is interesting to note the direction of writing by Williams and Francis, which is about walking together even in differences and working towards some level of harmony to avoid further violence. This has always been the way of thinking for indigenous peoples as well as many Asian nations including the Philippines. While colonialism still has its hold on many first-world and developing countries alike, this direction in writing and convergence on the idea of learning for the purpose of cultural change or ecological transformation are hopeful signs for the future—a future which, in Christian terms, is always about the kingdom of God (the *basileia tou theou*) where the wolf will dwell with the lamb under Jesus who is both the lion and the lamb, the conqueror and conquered/victim.[22] Under God's reign, the possibility of overcoming tribalism and colonialism become a reality. It is a reality that one works towards now, one that is hoped for in the future, and one that will certainly come in time.

* In saying this, Pope Francis has provided concrete steps towards the implementation of integral ecology and integral human development as shown in *Laudato Si* and more specifically in his *Message for the 104th world day of migrants and refugees*, in which he calls for the welcoming, protecting, promoting, and integrating of migrants. Thus, whilst he has provided concrete steps through such documents, Pope Francis admits, in *Laudato Si*, the challenges which inadvertently refer to tribalist mindsets: "Regrettably, many efforts to seek concrete solutions to the environmental crisis have proved ineffective, not only because of powerful opposition but also because of a more general lack of interest."

6

Mutual recognition

Kerry Pinkstone

Complex issues often seem intractable. Time and time again we feel close to making progress. We hold firm to our ideals. We feel optimistic that change is upon us, then we watch it slip through our fingertips and the moment passes us by. The status quo remains. We are stuck. We delay, we defer, and we divide when we should be looking for common ground and debating intelligently.

In his PM Glynn Lecture, Rowan Williams, former Archbishop of Canterbury, challenges his audience to confront the reality of political tribalism. He offers an account of political tribalism, and a way to overcome it if we are to protect the future of democracy while making progress on complex issues of national importance. Williams asserts that, if we are to move beyond political tribalism, and become unstuck, we shall need a "deeper literacy about our histories, a commitment to identifying the grammar of a common language and the work of negotiating a shared future by looking for solutions that have a degree of durability and credibility, even if they are no one's ideal".

There is no greater complexity of policy than in Indigenous affairs, particularly when it comes to the debate on constitutional recognition of Aboriginal and Torres Strait Islander peoples. I shall examine Williams's lecture in this context.

The Cape York leader, Noel Pearson, summarised the 'tribes' that exist in Indigenous affairs in his 2007 article, "Hunt for the radical centre":

> Australia is still divided into two ideological tribes.
>
> One tribe comprising most indigenous leaders and possibly most indigenous people (but by no means an overwhelming majority) and their progressive supporters holds the view that the absence or insufficient realisation of rights is the core of the indigenous predicament in our country.
>
> The other tribe comprises most non-progressive, non-indigenous Australians and their conservative political leaders (including substantial numbers in the Labor Party) who hold the view that it is the absence of responsibilities that lies at the core of our people's malaise.
>
> There is a third group comprising indigenous leaders such as me and ALP president Warren Mundine, who are trying to advocate a synthesis of the rights and responsibilities paradigms. I believe that a substantial proportion of ordinary indigenous people also believe that rights and responsibilities must be acknowledged and realised together. No such synthesis has coalesced and those seeking what I call the radical centre in this policy struggle are left straddling an ever-widening gulf between the two paradigms.

Indigenous people are not homogenous, and their views are diverse. Pearson's point is important as it demonstrates that political tribes naturally exist within the Indigenous community, in the same way as they do in the broader population.

Williams argues that the political debate in which your opponent is not merely mistaken, unwise, or uninformed, but malignant and/or sub-rational, is the gateway to majoritarian tyranny. The persistent booing of AFL player and Aboriginal man, Adam Goodes, is therefore worth consideration. Despite winning the prestigious Brownlow medal twice, Mr Goodes was booed every time he touched the ball in consecutive matches until eventually he quit playing altogether. The booing escalated after he called out an incident of racism, and started to speak up about racism in Australia. Mr Goodes was characterized by some as a whinger, a cheat, and a sook. He was even accused of vilifying the past and preaching division.[1]

Williams warns, however, that, by delegitimising the opponent in a debate, political tribalism is fertile seedbed for totalitarianism:

> It takes for granted that we don't need to rehearse the labour and negotiation, the difficulties, the false starts, by which moral and political perspectives are arrived at . . . because we don't need to see the perspective of the other as invested or developed . . . and resolve not to think of the other's view as sharing any of the moral anxieties or emotional tensions I experience.

The Australian journalist and Wiradjuri man, Stan Grant, made a powerful speech, "Racism and the Australian Dream", at the IQ2 debate in 2015. Mr Grant provided an insight into the moral anxieties and emotional tensions of the Goodes booing affair:

> Thousands of voices rose to hound an Indigenous man . . . they hounded that man into submission. I can't speak for what lay in the hearts of the people who booed Adam Goodes. But I can tell you what we heard when we heard those boos. We heard a sound that was very familiar to us . . . We heard a howl of humiliation that echoes across two centuries of dispossession, injustice, suffering and survival. We heard the howl of the Australian dream and it said to us again, you're not welcome.

Galarrwuy Yunupingu is a Yolngu* man and leader of the Gumatj clan in East Arnhem Land. He was Australian of the Year in 1978, is a Member of the Order of Australia, and has been named as one of Australia's National Living Treasures.

Yunupingu's 2008 article in the *Monthly* is another good example that shows these moral anxieties and emotional tensions are real and run very deep:

> the world of my father, the Yolngu world is always under threat, being swallowed up by whitefellas. This is a weight that is bearing down on me; it is a pressure that I feel now every moment of my life—it frustrates me and drives me crazy; at night it is like a splinter in my mind . . . I am a Gumatj man; I am fire; and that fire must burn until there is nothing left. That is what I have left to give to my family.[2]

Williams argues that a tribalised politics makes it increasingly difficult for participants to admit to having *learned* anything as this opens them up to looking vulnerable. Following the Goodes affair, how many fans now understand how the howling impacted not just Goodes himself, but the broader Indigenous community who felt silenced by the tyranny of the majority?

The avoidance of vulnerability drives us to "minimise the scope of this narrative to protracted learning, and to maximise the area of what is taken to be obviously and timelessly true". Williams asserts that learning occurs when sustainable habits encounter difficulty, frustration, and conflict, as this disequilibrium forces new habits to emerge.

Yunupingu talks openly about the Yolngu learning:

> Our allegiance is to each other, to our land and to the ceremonies

* Yolngu is the name of an Aboriginal nation consisting of thirteen clans of the Gove Peninsula in east Arnhem Land: Rirritjingu, Djapu, Wanguri, Djalwong, Mangalili, Malarrpa, Marrakulu, Dartiwuy, Naymil, Gumatj, Galpu, Djumbarrpi-ynu, Dhudi-Djapu.

> that define us. It is through the ceremonies that our lives are created. These ceremonies record and pass on the laws that give us ownership of the land and of the seas, and the rules by which we live. Our ceremonial grounds are our universities, where we gain the knowledge that we need . . . Without this learning, Yolngu can achieve nothing; they are nobody . . .
>
> My father sent me to school, although he worried that I might lose my Gumatj identity . . . As I received my education from my clan leaders and from the *balanda** teachers, I watched as the world changed. As I grew up I was recognised and set apart by my father . . . I dedicated myself, under the direction of my father and the older men, to a Yolngu future.

Yet Mr Yunupingu has had to respond to the disequilibrium he experienced and learnt to walk in two worlds—he is a Yolngu leader, while being an entrepreneur who is building economic independence and self-reliance for the Gumatj. He believes this protects their futures by building cattle stations, harvesting plantation timber, operating the healing centre, and negotiating with mining companies. His purpose is clear:

> This is about building our own lives, our own communities. If I can't give that opportunity to my clan, no one else can. What they achieve will be for them, out of their hard work, for their happiness and security—not for some outsider.

Our tolerance for learning and disruption is usually limited as we take what we see as a given to protect ourselves from looking vulnerable. For admitting to having learnt something is also an admission that our position was wrong or poorly informed. Political leaders, in a tribalised system of politics, fear this admission could undermine their authority and eventually lead to political death. Technical knowledge is required for learning to

* *Balanda* is the Yolngu word for a non-Indigenous person, originally used to describe a European person with whom the Yolngu traded prior to British colonisation.

begin, but only through deep human engagement can we truly overcome political tribalism.

To understand the unrelenting resilience and determination that Indigenous people have, despite the trauma that they have suffered, one can watch the *First Australians* documentary narrated by Arrernte and Kalkadoon filmmaker Rachel Perkins. Ms Perkins recounts true stories of black and white people during the British colonisation of Australia. Her ability to chronicle the collision of these two worlds gives the viewer the opportunity to engage in the deeper literacy about our histories that Williams argues is necessary to overcome political tribalism. Through the medium of filmmaking, Ms Perkins opens the minds of viewers, allowing them to think about these issues from a different perspective. Ms Perkins humanises the stories and gives viewers the ability to see how the historic injustices are inextricably linked to the political and policy challenges of today's communities.

Perkins's ability to engage the audience for the purpose of educating them is also on display in her 2019 Boyer Lectures, in which she encourages others to move outside their political tribes to "speak to an audience that isn't necessarily engaged in this topic" as "we can't just speak to our friends and family about this".[3]

Educational tools like *First Australians* or the Boyer lectures are the first rung on the ladder in overcoming political tribalism. But this alone will not allow new habits to emerge. For new habits to form, there must be deep engagement between political tribes that allows participants to build the mutual recognition necessary to achieve change. An important consideration in developing new habits, which requires us to legitimise the views of our tribal opponents, comes down to the language we use to communicate with one another.

As we seek to build a stronger nation, not necessarily a different nation, we can reflect on Williams's call for shared language. Williams says we shouldn't invent an entirely new language for this purpose, but find ways that enable us to "translate into terms that resonate". He is not asking participants to compromise their values entirely. Rather, the development of shared language should enable "a more protracted engagement on issues, an engagement that does not instantly turn into the naked contest of power". The shared language must be carefully thought through.

In 2017, the National Indigenous Constitutional Convention met at Uluru. It led to the Uluru Statement from the Heart. This was the first time a consensus had been articulated on the way Indigenous people would like to be recognised in the Australian Constitution. The Statement also contained a call for the creation of a Makarrata Commission to supervise the process of agreement-making between governments and First Nations.

The word 'Makarrata' is a Yolngu word from North East Arnhem land. Mr Yunupingu explained the term 'Makarrata' to Prime Minister Malcolm Turnbull at the 2017 Garma Festival in Arnhem Land:

> Now let me give you my final words: Yothu Yindi. Garma. Makarrata.
>
> These are very special words also. They mean coming together, working together, and making peace together.
>
> That is why this place is Garma. And this is the perfect place for us to find our path to a settlement. Our *wayawu*—our pathway through the bush.

Many people believe that Makarrata means 'treaty'. However, Gumatj woman, Merrikiyawuy Ganambarr-Stubbs, explains that 'Makarrata' has many layers of meaning. 'Makarrata' means a process of negotiation, rather than the outcome itself: "It can be a negotiation of peace, or a negotiation and an agreement where both parties agree to one thing so that there is no dispute or no other bad feeling".[4]

This is not the first time the term 'Makarrata' has been used. In 1987, in the lead up to the bicentenary, the Senate Standing Committee on Legal and Constitutional Affairs examined the possibility of a compact or 'Makarrata' between the Commonwealth and Indigenous Australians. The report was entitled, *Two Hundred Years Later*, but the idea of a treaty was rejected because of its connotations of an agreement between sovereign states, which is a concern still shared by many today.[5] The Australian Constitution Commission then rejected Indigenous recognition in the Constitution in 1988, citing a difficulty in reaching an agreed and appropriate set of words.

The 2018 Joint Select Committee on Constitutional Recognition Relating to Aboriginal and Torres Strait Islander Peoples re-examined this issue of Makarrata some thirty years later. Its final report stated:

> The Committee did not hear much evidence on Makarrata. To the extent that it did hear evidence on the idea of Makarrata, the Yolngu word was not well known among Aboriginal and Torres Strait Islander peoples. It also means different things to different people.

For Makarrata to succeed, a clear understanding of the language needs to be developed not just across the political spectrum, but within the Indigenous leadership, or else this component of the Uluru Statement from the Heart will risk being lost to political tribalism again.

If we truly want to overcome political tribalism, is simply developing shared language sufficient? When and how do we do the 'work' that Williams notes is necessary? I would argue there are two further considerations that must be taken into account.

The first consideration is defining purpose. Williams touches on this in his work, but it is fundamental to achieving any substantial progress on complex policy matters. Both purpose-driven approaches that are typically pro-active, and crisis-driven approaches that are re-active, allow participants to find common ground on an issue. However, once the crisis has subsided, there does not seem to be the level of will to maintain the efforts in the latter compared with the former. When a group comes together with a very strong sense of purpose, this will intrinsically inspire and motivate the participants, even when the external motivations no longer exist.

The second consideration is having an environment in which participants can do the deeper work that moves them beyond tribalism. Williams proposes "the construction of environments in which there is enough trust for such things to be articulated". The founder of the Center for Public Leadership at Harvard University's John F. Kennedy School of Government, Ron Heifetz, has developed a model of adaptive leadership.

Heifetz's model uses the term 'holding environments'. This is a deliberate means of bringing people together in a space that is both safe but uncomfortable. Heifetz argues people need to feel the tension of the issue in a way that allows them to learn, but not so much that the weight of the challenge will crush them and they disengage. This is a careful process that requires tension between participants for the purpose of learning.

In forums intended to overcome trauma or in judicial forums designed to achieve justice for victims, there is a strong emphasis on ensuring safety and minimising unnecessary discomfort. But when it comes to overcoming political tribalism, we need discomfort to enable change to occur. These moments of difficulty and conflict may also be generative, as Williams implores us to "grasp the history and structure of the 'investment' of the stranger" or else we "lose the sense that engagement . . . is a potential source of insight and enrichment."

Mr Yunupingu recounts the time when Malcolm Fraser visited Arnhem Land as prime minister. He had hoped to talk to the prime minister about the protection of Yolngu lands from mining, but there was not enough discomfort, in the right holding environment, using the common language:

> Fraser has asked us to fish with him, and we hope there are words we can say to him that will halt his changes to the land-rights laws and overturn the government's decision to mine at Ranger. But Fraser only thinks about the fish. The fish bite and Fraser starts to pull them in. "Look at this one!" he yells. I bait his line again. Toby is silent. "And again—a bigger one." He baits his own line now—getting the hang of it. "You beauty, a barramundi!" All the time I try and put words in his mind about the importance of land, about the importance of respect, about giving things back in a proper way, not a halfway thing. But he has his mind on other things—he's not listening; he doesn't have to. He just keeps catching barramundi, enjoying himself.

Mr Yunupingu later admits the solutions to the future have become harder and harder to grasp, and from his experience, nothing is ever what it seems.

Discomfort drives change.

In tribal politics, we should recognise that what is uncomfortable to one group may feel very different to another. And, to overcome political tribalism, there should be a recognition that political safety goes both ways. What provides political safety to Indigenous stakeholders would seem politically unsafe to politicians, and vice versa. These vulnerabilities will not be quantitatively different—in that you can not rank them as more or less important than those experienced by someone else. They are qualitatively different, and therefore must be considered by different participants in order to truly experience the mutual recognition Williams speaks of.

Williams argues that we need to try to understand where our political opponents are coming from, but we have to understand that this space we create is going to have to deal with different vulnerabilities for the different parties to overcome political tribalism and leave identity politics behind in order to make progress. He emphasises that it requires all parties to consider this as a two-way process.

This is one of the ongoing challenges in constitutional reform. It can be difficult to create the holding environments that are both politically safe and suitably uncomfortable, especially when you are dealing with political leaders and decision-makers. It is a fact that Indigenous Australians are only 3% of Australia's population, and are further disempowered because of this extreme minority status.

Williams argues that democratic majorities establish what the majority of citizens seek and therefore recognise as lawful, requiring minorities to abide by these rules. This is true of Aboriginal and Torres Strait Islander peoples, who are an extreme minority. History shows their voices have not been heard.

Williams makes the point that democratic majorities cannot establish what is true or good, and therefore rely on working democracies to make provision for the "liberty of conscience". It is this liberty of conscience that we must rely on if we are to make progress in addressing the substantial disadvantage and structural disempowerment Indigenous people face in this nation.

Rachel Perkins recognises the losses that come as a result of tribal politics:

> Being present at all these opportunities that were lost; whether that be the bicentennial, which was the celebration of 200 years of European occupation, or in 2000 with the statement of

> reconciliation rejected, or the anniversary of the 1967 referendum in 2017, I've just been part of all these pushes, to get people to reckon with the history and past of Indigenous people.

It is imperative that we overcome political tribalism to avoid missing out on the opportunity to build a stronger, fairer nation, and a Constitution that reflects in a substantive way the desire of Indigenous people to be heard. We can no longer remain stuck in a paradigm where tribal politics triumphs at the expense of human growth and learning.

Williams offers a way to overcome tribal politics, and it is now up to all of us to find common ground on these very serious and important national issues. It is uncomfortable work, but it is necessary work if we want to create a stronger nation where every citizen of Australia feels valued.

7

ORIENTALISM, LEARNING AND TRIBALIST VIOLENCE

AUSTIN WYATT

> In the beginning, we create the enemy. Before the weapon comes the image. We think others to death and then invent the battle-axe or ballistic missiles with which to actually kill them. Propaganda precedes technology.
>
> Sam Keen, *Faces of the Enemy*[1]

When we consider the development of the modern political order, it becomes clear that humanity has generally failed to coexist and compromise without the resort to political violence, a phenomenon that is intertwined with the continued role of tribalism in the public consciousness. As any opponent of genetically modified crops will tell you, there is value in diversity and danger in promoting homogeneity to the exclusion of alternatives. However, as Rowan Williams notes, the post-Enlightenment Western identity is underpinned by an enduring sense of seemingly timeless modernity; a superiority of purpose that, by contrast, condemns those outside the 'tribe' as relics of another age; bypassed by the 'natural' march of progress and doomed to extinction.[2]

It is this sense that the Enlightenment model of society, with its technocratic structure and individualist focus, is the natural end-state of civilisational development, and that by reaching this end-state Western states are somehow superior to differently organised societies, which nurtures the exclusionary rhetoric and practices which in turn lead to inter-tribal violence.

While this view of Western society as the end state of societal development is problematic for those opposed to violence, it did not emerge overnight or in isolation. Rather, the development of Western forms of identity has been shaped in part by the parallel development of a class of peoples who are separated through discourse, against whom the prosecution of warfare takes on a distinctly unrestrained nature. Certainly part of this phenomenon is the result of the enduring connection between Western (Occidental) identity and an antagonistic (often Eastern or Oriental) Other, which can be traced back to ancient Greece.[3] However, its continuation into the modern era owes more to the—largely unwitting—contribution of the early orientalist scholars. Though believing themselves to be conducting objective, impartial inquiry, by focusing on the cultural, political, and linguistic asymmetries between their own society and those which they studied, these scholars were in fact building the basis of a discourse that legitimised violence and oppression of other political tribes as exotic, irrational, threatening, and underdeveloped.

Therefore, far from a neutral academic framework, orientalist studies evolved in such a manner that it contributed to sustaining a discourse that attributed the longstanding cultural antagonism between Europe and the 'East'; to perceived cultural, social, and political asymmetries, which were in turn believed to be the result of a fundamentally irrational or underdeveloped society.[4] In 1975,

Edward Said, a pioneer of postcolonial studies, released his book *Orientalism* (subsequently expanded upon in the 1985 paper, "Orientalism Revisited"), in which he critiqued this process and argued that scholars of the East had contributed to, and been shaped by, imperialist structures of power and discourse.

Orientalism establishes the concept of an inferior and irrational, and therefore dangerous, 'Other' who stands as the true antagonist of European identity. Oriental cultures are considered malformed, and in need of guiding by the firm hand of the more evolved Europeans.[5] This framework of thought justified a form of cultural imperialism, but its impact went beyond imperial administration, and can be seen in approaches to warfare.[6] The Other is feared, despised, demeaned, and suppressed; not reasoned with or treated with the dignity afforded to 'civilised' combatants.[7] The grand words of treaties are undermined by a culture of fear and misunderstanding.[8] The Other is every threat, real or imagined, that the laws of war aim to keep at bay.[9]

Orientalist discourse creates 'the Other', who is fundamentally flawed and unable to be understood or reasoned with. Rather, the Other is to be despised, feared, and demeaned, and its culture studied and suppressed. While the impact of European imperialism has been thoroughly explored in other works, this essay focuses on exploring the impact of orientalist scholarship as a legitimising feature of orientalist discourse on the conduct of warfare against 'oriental' societies and argues that the lessons of these early incidents are highly applicable to current conflicts.

The main impact of orientalism is to provide an ontological foundation for the perceived psychological and cultural divide between the Western/First World and their Oriental rivals.[10] Early orientalists certainly contributed to creating the narrative basis for this divide, even unintentionally, through their categorisation and separation of the East. As the core contributors of the civil sphere, the section of society that produces culture (artists, writers, philosophers etc),[11] orientalist scholars exercised influence beyond their ivory towers over the economic, military, and political spheres. Overall, therefore, despite purporting to provide objective analysis, these scholars were contributing to a self-reinforcing academic orthodoxy that perpetuated the assumptions that underpinned orientalist discourse.

Furthermore, Said argues that orientalism, particularly its new American form, exists within a self-perpetuating discourse that is reinforced by cultural drivers (including movies, books, and video games). These drivers indoctrinate the population into the oriental discourse, as they internalise and reproduce orientalist attitudes. It is noteworthy that even the ancient Greeks left evidence of depictions of the Persians in their plays and writings that indicated what scholars would later recognise as orientalism. Consider the number of modern entertainment items that feature Arab, Muslim, or fundamentalist villains; compare this to the preponderance of Soviet/Russian villains in entertainment media during the Cold War. By adding to the orientalist discourse, such cultural mechanisms contribute to the separation that allows Western democratic governments greater leeway to impose force, undertake mass surveillance, and even undertake targeted killings.[12]

However, it is also important not to lose sight of the fact that the true success of orientalism occurs when members of the Other population begin to 'self-other'. This process occurs when members of the oriental society, usually those who are prominent or wealthy, consciously adopt conspicuous Western traits and are complicit in accepting their culture's oriental status.[13] This could be seen particularly clearly in nineteenth and twentieth-century European imperial possessions, such as India, where wealthy colonised subjects sent their children to prominent Western schools in order to integrate them into the allegedly superior

Western culture. When a culture self-orientalises it accepts the imposition of this distinctly Western discourse, with the implicit lower status of the Oriental, further ingraining its influence upon both the Occidental and Oriental societies.

At the peak efficiency of orientalism, the Other becomes sufficiently dehumanised that both soldiers and civilians begin to see that group as subhuman, animalistic, and prosecutable.[14] While the archetypical Other for the average American has shifted over the last eighty years from the Japanese, to the Communists, to the Islamic Fedayeen,[15] each was demonized and marginalised at home and abroad. In this process, Said argues that scholars and institutions of learning are not blameless. How these groups are studied and categorised by the civil sphere, he argues, has a powerful impact on how the Other is perceived in the broader society. It is this altered perception that then allows states far greater leeway to exercise violence against that group. Suitably separated from the targeted group, the majority of Western civilians do not question the methods taken in the name of their safety; instead, we sit calmly in the belly of the Leviathan while it kills our neighbours.

Rowan Williams begins his lecture on political tribalism with the remark that "to speak of 'tribalism' or of 'tribal' attitudes and behaviour is to mark out certain kinds of human behaviour as aberrations from the norm. These behaviours may be intriguing, even sympathetic in certain ways, but they are ultimately both doomed and deviant". Among the key characteristics of modern states is the monopoly on the legitimate use of force; when this interacts with the tribalism that Williams describes, there is the risk that this 'other' will be subjected to violence as a way of protecting the societal 'body'. Understanding the interaction between this process, the Other, and Orientalist discourse requires an explanation of biopolitics and state power.

While discussions of violence and the exercise of force are generally focused on the power to end life, the twentieth-century French philosopher, Michel Foucault, argued instead that power in modern states is exercised through control *over life.*[16] At a societal level, biopower is the exercise of power through the control over life, using disciplinary power and discourse to manage behaviour and the societal structure of a society.[17] Biopower utilises control over life to ensure compliance, separating and punishing individuals who demonstrate deviant behaviours.

Those that deviate from the expected behaviours or threaten the state are relegated to a situation of bare life, where political value is stripped from the lives of those within the Othered group. Under this paradigm, the Other can be thought of as an exile under the law, existing within a state of exemption[18] and liable to forcible subjugation to the state's sovereign will. Their lives can be killed but are never 'sacrificed'.[19] Giorgio Agamben (an Italian contemporary of Foucault) states that the Western state's unrestricted ability to end the lives of such individuals forms the basis of its sovereign power.[20] Violence under biopower is bureaucratised and impersonal,[21] with targets identified through their deviant behaviours.[22] The identity of the individual deviant is irrelevant; their behaviour marks them as a threat to the health of the societal body. Thus, the deviant is separated from the body and destroyed.

State violence under a biopower regime commonly includes an element of racism; with force being used to protect the societal 'body' from the biological threat posed by specific other groups.[23] By eliminating members of other 'races', the society exercises its power to purify and strengthen itself though the extermination of its rivals.[24] The Ismalis were a fiercely independent sect that separated from Nizari Shiite Muslims. Their use of assassination as a tool of state power is a clear example of biopolitical racism informing the decision to use violence against individuals outside of the societal body. What scholars have been able to prove about the Ismalis' methodology speaks of a non-individualistic, highly symbolic approach to assassination; one in which the death of the target is the primary but not sole goal. In a manner that will resonate with scholars of modern terrorist organisations, small groups of Ismalis would strike their targets in broad daylight and always with knives, which had the secondary effect of creating a public spectacle. While the perpetrators were not fundamentally on a suicide mission, they were willing to die to accomplish their task. Their victims were chosen, not because of who they were or in retaliation for their actions, but because they were the leaders of rival tribes that threatened the Ismalis. Agents of the societal body were thus applying violence as a way to purify the perceived tribe (in cases of internal violence) or to eliminate perceived external threats to the 'body'.

Beyond the Ismalis, history has shown that states have consistently exercised less restrained levels of coercive force and even violence against those outside the majority's 'tribe' without effective public backlash. To understand why this process occurs, and how it is justified within societies whose citizens largely consider themselves to be ethically good, we must take a step back and consider the role of discursive power.

Discourse is a collection of concepts, composed of ideas, attitudes, courses of action, beliefs, and practices that systematically construct the subjects and the worlds of which they speak. At one point in his reflections on discourse, Williams says, "Shared languages certainly don't necessitate shared views; but they enable a more protracted engagement on issues, an engagement that does not instantly turn into the naked contest of power." Discourse operates as this shared language within, and sometimes between, political tribes and is, therefore, an essential factor to consider in any understanding of relations of power. This is particularly true in the case of biopower, where it produces the social relations for authority and conformity. Discourse maintains the externally focused, segregated, racial societies that form the core of the biopolitical model. Discourse allows individuals and groups to be severed from the societal body and reclassified. Through discourse, the actions of one individual are no longer merely a breach of law; rather, they are symptoms of deviance. Once identified as deviant, the individual becomes subject to a "series of descriptive statements" that identifies the individual with a deviant class.[25] The labels 'terrorist', 'criminal', and 'extremist' all set up a pattern of language that immediately excludes the individual from society. This process is subjugating in that it reinforces a particular type of speech around the subsequent action while limiting others in order to legitimise the use of state violence. When this occurs, political tribalism arises: as Williams explains, "Political tribalism is above all a shrinkage of the scope of mutual recognition: I resolve not to think of the other's view as sharing any of the moral anxieties or emotional tensions I experience."

As Williams points out, however, tribalism is a multi-actor phenomenon:

> What's more, it is—again, naturally enough—seen as imperfectly human, so that life lived within these terms is less than it should be, less than the fullness that we now enjoy and have grown into. Non-modern life is a *deprived* life, so that the efforts to eradicate it can be seen as part of a struggle for fullness of human experience—the struggle that shows we are, in the odd but persistent phrase, 'on the side of history.'

So it is important to consider how alternative tribal identities also influence international relations and violence in the modern era. There is not a single 'eastern' occidentalism, which in itself speaks to the institutional biases in academia explored by postcolonial scholars. For the purposes of this essay, it is sufficient to turn to the concept of occidentalism that was fittingly established as a companion view to orientalism. As with its more well-known counterpart, the Occident refers to the imagined community of 'the West', rather than an objectively established list of societies. That is not to say that there isn't a generally agreed view of which states fall within the West, it is more to note that there are real, practical consequences in how states associated with this term are perceived. Professor Jonathan Spencer, a social anthropologist at the University of Edinburgh, argues that in a non-westerner's view, the West is overtaken by an obsession with rationality, which stems from the Enlightenment.[26] The dominant characteristic, therefore, is that Western societies are fundamentally utilitarian in nature, being able to justify negative (even immoral) actions through self-rationalisation. Finnish historical ethnologists Jouhki Jukka and Henna-Riikka Pennanen present occidentalism as a similar perspective to orientalism, but distinguish it on the basis of a more defensive or reactive stance.

While not corresponding directly to orientalism, it is also worth considering how alternative exercises of discursive power have been leveraged by Eastern states to challenge the liberal normative framework and to promote loyalty to the societal 'body'.[27] The earliest example of this effect can be seen in ancient Persia, where those who did not subscribe to their ethno-religious viewpoint are described in de-legitimising terms that would have been familiar to their Greek neighbours. By distinguishing and denigrating those outside of their culture, the Persian elite was able to leverage tribalism to secure their own societal order and prevent intrusion by outside influences.[28] As a more contemporary example, consider the emergence of 'civilisational state' discourse among Chinese and Russian policymakers and certain scholars. The civilisational state is distinguished from, and portrayed in opposition to, the nations states of the West. As an example, consider how Xi Jinping has capitalised on the message that

China must return to the world stage as a global power after their "century of humiliation".[29] At the same time, Chinese civilisational discourse enshrines a dichotomy between Chinese culture and the "barbarism"[30] and moral decay that is perceived to characterize Western states.[31] By promoting the importance of conservative values and leveraging a narrative of usurpation and exploitation by the West, this discourse contributes to a conceptually similar form of normative exceptionalism to that of the Enlightenment Western identity.

While this essay, as with William's lecture, chooses to focus on the post-Enlightenment, orientalist conception of the Western identity as the final point of cultural evolution, the discourse of identity has proven a powerful tool for motivating violence for political ends across quite distinct tribes. At the pinnacle of this negative process, regardless of the terminology, is the development of the Other, which comprises both a deviant group and an opposing race whose form shifts with political requirements.

At the core of understanding the interaction between Western tribalism, the Other, and violence is the understanding that Western identity in this context has developed with reference to a perpetual antagonistic force. Even as the first European and the Mediterranean tribes came into being, this us-them distinction became deeply ingrained in their methods of war and political discourse. The European warrior was constructed as an honourable combatant fighting for a noble cause, while the Oriental fighter was decried as criminal, allowing the Western state to disregard the rules of 'civilised' combat. Even when this Othered combatant adopted comparable weapons, doctrine, or tactics to those of their Western counterparts, orientalist discourse provided an ostensibly objective rationale for still excluding them from the rules of combat. As a result of this, exceptions developed alongside even the earliest codes of armed conduct, justified by a philosophical, legal, or cultural argument based on an assertion of illegitimacy.

While this concept of an illegitimate combatant, unentitled to protections by nature and separated from the 'civilised' soldier by nature of seemingly objective analysis of cultural asymmetry, can be traced back at least as far as organised inter-tribal warfare.[32] For the sake of this analysis it is sufficient to begin with the classical ancient civilisations. It is important to note here that Edward Said traces orientalism to the culture of fifth-century Greece.[33] Said points to Aeschylus' Persians as a precursor for the motif of the East as an insinuating danger, undermining the rationality of the European (Greek) civilisation. Consider how the story of 300 Spartans defending the cradle of Western democracy against the Persians at Thermopylae continues to be celebrated in popular culture, despite the fact that Sparta was a highly regimented, monarchical city-state, which would become embroiled in the ruinous Peloponnesian War against Athens roughly fifty years later.

Moving forward to the next bastion of Western identity, the Roman legionnaire was portrayed as shielding the light of civilisation against hordes of uncivilised barbarians. This view, which was particularly prominent during the Enlightenment, minimised the fact that Rome was an expansionist power that subsumed those same 'barbarians' through romanisation, a process of cultural elimination and assimilation, which was widely believed to be of benefit to the uncivilised barbarian tribes. As Williams states in relation to Canadian 'native schools': "Genocide can wear the dress of benign progressivism, *as well as* that of murderous violence." While these were among the earliest examples of the interaction between political tribalism and violence toward groups deemed external, they were far from the only instances.

The first concept that comes to mind when considering warfare in the middle ages is chivalry, with its ideal of noble knights in shining armour facing off in honourable combat. The evidence, however, suggests that chivalry was never applied to combat against lower classes or non-Christians. The Teutonic Order's campaign against pagans in Eastern Europe included the liberal use of hostages, attacks on civilians, and torture,[34] and the Spanish Reconquista wiped out the Muslim population of the Iberian Peninsula.[35] This is to say nothing of the Crusades, in which knights and lower-class soldiers were given religious justification for committing the most heinous war crimes, with a particularly notable incident being the Sack of Jerusalem in 1099. The state and the Catholic Church indoctrinated the European population with a blatantly untrue and damning view of the Muslim world, particularly in the wake of the Mongol incursion in 1241.[36] In order to avoid conflict within Christendom, the elites installed the belief of the Other as an existential threat to society that had to be justifiably exterminated.[37]

It is also worth noting the interaction between the development of the concept of 'just war' during this period and warfare against those outside of Christendom.[38] A clear example of this interaction can be seen with the crossbow. While crossbows had been used during the Roman era, their use in medieval armies was condemned. This was largely because mass-produced crossbows were the first weapon that gave the lowliest peasant the reliable capability to kill the warrior elite, the knight class, without extensive training.[39] Primarily because of the threat it posed to the established power structure, crossbows were twice banned by the Catholic Church as an unfit weapon for civilised combat.[40] However, this ban was not applied in wars declared 'just' by the Catholic Church; typically this meant against Muslims or other 'heretics'.[41] They featured extensively in crusading armies, with the consent of the church. Most major powers ignored the ban and even the church employed crossbowmen.[42] Eventually, crossbows began to filter back into European mainstream armies,[43] and Richard the Lionheart was killed while suppressing a revolt in

1199 by a crossbow bolt fired by a child.*

The Ismalis, who were also active during this period, had a far-reaching impact on orientalism. Despite more recent critical research by a number of modern scholars including Komel, Daftary and Belfield, there remains a disturbing proportion of academics, beyond just neo-orientalists, who continue to believe and promote the myths surrounding this sect, to the extent that they are far better known as Hashashin.[44]

According to the popular understanding, the Hashashin were a sect of deadly, fanatical Islamic assassins who unquestionably served the 'Old Man of the Mountain'. They protected their isolated mountain keep (Alamut) against powerful empires and crusading armies by the liberal application of terror and the use of highly trained assassins who were more than willing to die after completing their task, often making no effort to escape capture after a successful kill. The myth attributes this seemingly irrational disregard for their personal safety to the use of some form of narcotic, allegedly cannabis. This claim is based on the fact that the Arabic form of the English term 'assassin' is 'hashishiyyun', which literally means the users of hashish (cannabis), a scorn laid upon the Nizari by the Sunni.[45] By the time it became popularised in 1818, 'assassin' had become the English term for political murderer simply by virtue of association with a mistranslated slur.

A mysterious order of Eastern Islamic killers that fanatically followed the commands of their leader, who further secured their loyalty with narcotics and promises of paradise, was clearly fertile ground for orientalists. Much of what we popularly attribute to the Ismalis was actually created by early orientalists. An example is their supposed maxim "nothing is true, everything is permitted", which was traced to 1838, over five hundred years

* At the time he was struck, Richard I was laughing at another crossbowman who had been using a frying pan to protect himself from arrows: M. Evans, *The Death of Kings: Royal Deaths in Medieval England* (A&C Black, 2007), p. 8.

after the order had been wiped out. Interestingly, this slogan was extremely popular in nineteenth-century newspapers and journals to smear atheists, a strange choice of slogan for a supposed highly religiously indoctrinated organisation. Furthermore, the central role marijuana allegedly played in securing loyalty was calculated to create immediate uproar because of the very negative perception of drugs in Western communities and the perception that drugs and disease were imported from the Eastern, or periphery, states. The assassin has played different roles in contemporary literature, but what is immediately noteworthy is the level to which obviously fictionalised historical novels influenced serious public and academic assumptions about the order.

Returning to Europe, the age of musketry was a period of great societal change, which saw the rise of nationalism and arguably the first instance of total war. Europe in the late eighteenth century was still characterized by the aftermath of the American and later French revolutions; rebellions of the lower classes (and colonists) fomented around dangerous concepts of liberty and the removal of the nobility had toppled one of the greatest European powers (France) and thoroughly damaged the prestige of another (England). The Other rears its head in the propaganda of revolutionary France, which demanded that citizens of the new French Republic viciously and proactively protect it by seeking out moderates, monarchists, and separatists who threatened the revolution simply by existing.[46] The region of Vendee provided them with all three of these 'vile' supposedly counter-revolutionary groups, who were subjected to a severe and very bloody punitive campaign in which French Republican 'Hell Columns' killed approximately 100,000 civilians. Men, women, and children of all faiths and political persuasions were killed in this campaign, portrayed as acceptable casualties by the assertion that it was a legitimate campaign of proactive self-defence against traitors and rebels.

The Vendee atrocities were committed against the backdrop of increasingly violent revolutionary wars. Those who fought for the other European powers were portrayed as repressors locked in the service of the past. Compare this to the French National Guardsmen, who fought without shoes and often with a pike because of an acute musket shortage. They were portrayed as citizen-soldiers protecting the rights of their fellow citizen against the backward Ancien Régime. However, the Other always plays both sides; soldiers of the major European powers believed that they were stopping the erosion of Christian values and legitimate monarchism, which was based on a divine right to rule. There were clear echoes of this during the Cold War. The revolutionary conflicts are fascinating because they are one of the few instances in which both sides willingly and publicly threw aside the rules of war. This was particularly true in the eighteenth-century Italian campaigns against the 'vicious Turk'.[47]

The spread of European imperialism in the eighteenth and early nineteenth centuries also marked the beginning of the relationship between orientalism and the excesses of empire. This relationship can be traced to Napoleon, who led a doomed expedition to Egypt. While this expedition was mostly an opportunity for Napoleon to firm his support base through military success and to cut England off from India, it also secured an opportunity for orientalists and other scholars to comprehensively raid Egypt's rich cultural heritage. During the French occupation of Egypt, Napoleon demonstrated a conciliatory approach to Islam, condemning Voltaire's depiction of Muhammad as a fanatic and proclaiming publicly that he was a true Muslim. Prioritising good relations with the locals, Napoleon banned his soldiers from drinking and enforced a strict code of conduct. He also drew up battle plans for a conquering march through Persia along the overland route to India. Writing after his exile to St Helena, Napoleon described an enduring vision he had of himself astride an elephant, bearing a new version of the Quran, as his troops established a French-controlled Caliphate. Despite clear respect for Islam, which extended to the point that some historians have suggested that the strongly anti-Catholic Napoleon converted to Islam during his time in Egypt, it is important to note that he also ignored the rules of civilised warfare against the Mamelukes. After the Siege of Jaffa, 4,500 prisoners were executed.[48] This incident went largely unremarked, however, because Napoleon and his contemporaries regularly broke what modern scholars would consider the laws of armed conflict during the bitter Napoleonic Wars. Out of the fires of the Napoleonic Wars the spectre of nationalism rose in Europe, subsequently spreading across their empires.

For the Europeans, the fear of Islamic nationalism infecting vital colonial possessions trumped the widespread belief in the orientalist false-assertion of Islamic backwardness. During the nineteenth century, this fear manifested in repressive colonial policies and war crimes.[49] The Europeans were indoctrinated in the orientalist belief that disciplining the oppressed colonial populations was part of the white man's burden; a vital component in ostensibly benevolent efforts to raise them to the level of Europeans. The general consensus remained, however, that African and Asian societies were un-evolved sub-humans unentitled to the consideration or protection warranted to a European non-combatant.

The colonies became the testing ground for weapons and tactics that were deemed uncivilised for use on European combatants. For example, early machine guns were primarily used on indigenous populations.[50] Imperial powers even blocked attempts to expand the laws of war though conventions that prohibited the use of certain weaponry, a clear example being the British refusal to join a ban on expanding ammunition solely because it was considered to be more effective at stopping the proverbial charging native warrior. Rebellions were punished severely by Europeans in order to deter other colonies from attempting revolt.

As an example of this interaction in the colonial era, consider the evolution of military aircraft. Among their earliest uses was to conduct punitive strikes against unruly colonial subjects, such as the 1912 French 'police action' in Morocco that targeted villages and herds of livestock.[51] The first aerial bombardment occurred in 1911, when an Italian pilot took to dropping hand grenades on Ottoman trenches. However, this attracted widespread criticism at the time and aerial warfare against Europeans was deemed unacceptable.[52]

As a result, systematic bombardment was largely confined to use against colonial populations. Consider the Rules of Aerial Warfare, adopted in 1923, which specifically prohibited aerial bombardment of civilian targets with the primary objective of causing terror or intimidation. However, when the French killed over 1,000 civilians in a single air raid on Damascus in 1925, protests lodged with the international community by Syrian authorities were dismissed and the French claimed that the prohibition on bombarding undefended towns did not apply outside of Europe.[53] Officially, this sort of colonial air bombardment was often called 'policing actions' against 'bandits' and 'uncivilised' tribesmen who were not covered by the laws of war.

Early use of air power by colonial powers certainly did not merit the title 'police action'. In 1919, the British used a targeted bombing campaign to subdue the Mad Mullah of Somaliland*, who had never even seen an aeroplane. Following three days of bombardment, the Mullah surrendered. In the 1920s, the European

* Mohammed Abdille Hassan (the Mad Mullah of Somaliland) was a prominent Ethiopian religious and political leader who established the Dervish state (Gray, 1980, p. 41). He proved to be a persistent challenger to British colonial rule. Several prior punitive land expeditions had failed to kill him or subdue his forces (Lindqvist, *A history of bombing*, p. 50). He died of influenza a few months after surrendering (Hess, 1964, p. 432).

air forces conducted punitive strikes using anti-personnel shrapnel bombs and white phosphorus.* The devastating British aerial 'occupation' of Iraq replaced land forces with punitive aerial raids, causing thousands of deaths. Only Sweden (who had prior interests in Ethiopia), protested against the remarkably brutal Italian campaign against Ethiopia in the early 1930s, which included indiscriminate bombardment and the use of poison gas against civilians.

The comprehensive lack of discrimination in the use of force was attributed to the backward nature of the targeted populace. Local tribes were often characterized as loving to fight for fighting's sake, and as regarding those who discriminated between combatants and non-combatants as weak. Military action against the Other was romanticised and separated from existing standards of morality, which encouraged the use of new or otherwise unacceptable weapon systems. An interesting by-product of the European reliance on airpower was the frequent claim that colonial authorities should avoid allowing the locals to gain familiarity with aircraft, in the belief that as long as the locals did not understand how aircraft worked they would continue to view them as vessels of 'divine retribution'.[54]

The colonial period was the apogee of classical orientalism's influence upon the conduct of European war against the Other. The above are merely a small selection of a much larger parade of atrocities committed by the 'civilised' Europeans against the oriental, typically Muslim, antagonist.

Rowan Williams reminds us that aberrant tribal identities

---

* Arthur Harris (later to gain fame as 'Bomber' Harris in the Second World War) was a squadron commander in Iraq. In an official report from the RAF to Parliament, he claimed the British campaign was effective because "They [Iraqis] now know that within forty-five minutes a full-sized village can be practically wiped out and a third of its inhabitants killed or injured by four or five machines which offer them no real target, no opportunity for glory as warriors, no effective means of escape" (Lindqvist, *A history of bombing*, p. 57).

> are ultimately both doomed and deviant; they are forms of life that are, at best, noble but destined for extinction. And the rational and 'normal' dominant group will, where necessary, with whatever appropriate expressions of regret, act as the agents of fate, and accelerate this extinction by one or another form of genocide.

The Other, particularly the Islamic Other, has always been a source of misunderstanding and fear for European and, by extension, Western societies.[55] When people fear the unknown, they give up their liberties to the Leviathan in exchange for protection. While Europe and America were the centres for the genesis of badly needed rules for the conduct of warfare, these same states were consistently working to undermine their implementation by perpetually excluding the Oriental. Though purporting to be producing objective analysis, Western scholars, largely unintentionally, cultivated the assumption that the Oriental was inferior, in some cases subhuman. This assumption allowed Western generals not to apply the rules of civilised combat in conflicts with Oriental cultures, particularly the on-going conflict with Islamic extremist groups. At every point between the ancient world and the early colonial period, Western states have justified appalling conduct under the shadow of the white man's burden. It is therefore no surprise that the fruits of this enduring historical paradigm are the suicide bombers of today.

8

DIGITAL TRIBALISM

ETHAN WESTWOOD

The world is rapidly moving towards a digitally saturated future. The digital space persists in all the niches, large or small, in our society. Much of our daily life has transferred into this space as information, entertainment, and political commentary, along with much else, have all been digitised.

News is now found online. Print newspaper sales are in decline and draw closer to their fate as a commodity of the past. Television and cinema have been replaced by streaming services and video-sharing platforms such as YouTube which boasts a user base of two billion users. Political commentary has also shifted further from traditional media as internet talk shows become centres for political influence. We no longer need separate means to consume information and content. It is all held and consolidated within technology owned by nearly everyone.

Digital media can be accessed anywhere at any time. For the most part, it comes at no monetary expense to the consumer. Thus, the digital space has been successfully integrated into the lives of most people. Younger generations and those raised with the growth of the digital space have never known any different. Integration with the digital space is something that is almost natural to the young and future generations will only be further integrated. The way in which society experiences and consumes media is increasingly digitised and this will persist as an important feature of how individuals go about their lives.

The digital space and its algorithmic foundations have features that can be utilised in ways that are not possible in the physical space. This has unique consequences for political tribalism. Political tribalism, according to Rowan Williams, occurs when individuals perceive their shared opinion as being the only rational agenda. This attitude allows individuals to consider other opinions inferior, when, in fact, it is just that they are different. Conflict arises between groups who each believe that they alone have reached the correct conclusion about the problem, and that all others' ideas or solutions are irrational. The conflict begins with discussion and debate, but risks descending into threats of violence, supremacy, and mobilisation to assert the dominance of one particular way of thinking. The digital space has an innate ability to alter, amplify, and accelerate many things. It is an exceptionally fertile ground for concepts and ideas, increasing their potency in a way that is not possible in the physical space. This unique environment has new implications for Williams's notion of political tribalism.

These implications could be considered assets of the digital space. It offers great possibilities for learning and communication. It is associated with liberty, unbridled expression, and creativity. These freedoms can allow for many instances of constructive progress in society, and can be utilised as a tool that can greatly assist in overcoming political tribalism. The digital space can provide an amplified version of learning. In theory, one can find information about any event, opinion, or person, and learn in a much more efficient manner, without needing to purchase books or travel to libraries. One can be enriched by the cultures and opinions of others which would never have been encountered in the physical space. The digital space also offers unprecedented methods of communication between nearly anyone anywhere. Distances between locations are no longer a barrier. People can contact someone on the other side of the globe without having to move away from their devices. One can have the opportunity to engage in dialogue with individuals of any and all backgrounds and come to discuss similarities and differences between them. The level of exposure to other ways of thinking is nearly incalculable. These features suggest that the digital space should assist in overcoming political tribalism. They serve as opportunities for the learning that Williams outlines as essential for that purpose. Simply having the ability to access information anywhere, whether through sites or directly from another person, gives individuals the opportunity to come to understand other worldviews as also being equally rational as one's own worldview. As such, the digital space can bring about new possibilities for overcoming political tribalism.

Alas, those sentiments are strictly idealistic. The digital space, in its current form, actually creates a new obstacle to overcoming political tribalism. It is not simply a benign space with new features that lead to new possibilities. Rather, some of its new features lead to new problems. The way in which the digital space is structured and curated does not allow for the cultivation of liberty and exploration as anticipated above. Such notions simply cover up the true way in which the digital space is curated and controlled. The way in which the digital space seems is in direct contrast with the way it actually is. It is controlled by algorithms, not human agency. To most users, these algorithms are incomprehensible strings of numbers and letters. But those strings of code control each individual experience in the digital space. They hide the way in which the digital space can isolate and divide those who spend time within it. It has specific ways in which it can create distinct parallel worlds that entrap users in intellectual echo chambers. In the same way that the digital space connects anyone anywhere, it can just as easily isolate anyone anywhere, causing greater detrimental effects than other forms of communication between individuals who hold opposing beliefs ever could have. This phenomenon is known as 'filter bubbles', and the trouble comes when users find themselves perpetually trapped within them.

Filter bubbles were first discussed by Eli Pariser, an internet activist and author of *The Filter Bubble: What The Internet Is Hiding From You*, which provided much of the basis for discussion about the bubbles. Filter bubbles are defined by Pariser as personal intellectual environments that conform to a user's preferences as a result of algorithms unknown to the user. These algorithms measure and gather information including a user's previous searches on a search engine, physical locations of the user, type of devices used, and also links and advertisements clicked on, so that the algorithm can tailor future content specifically to align with those previous choices and interests. In this way, algorithms influence future search results, personalised news streams, social media streams, and targeted advertisements, along with many other things that a user will see while in the digital space. Everything that a user encounters while exploring the digital space will have been curated as a consequence of the algorithms, in a way that ensures that the user's specific worldview is affirmed rather than challenged. Users can, therefore, become intellectually and culturally trapped, as the algorithms lead them to engage only with content which, and communicate only with individuals who, share their opinions and ideas. This effectively isolates users. They are unlikely to engage in a dialogue with other users who have different opinions and ideas, as there is no opportunity presented to them to move beyond their respective filter bubbles.

This problem is genuinely new: nothing has ever been seen

like it before. There is not an explicit choice that a user makes to enter the bubble. It is different from situations in the past, in which an individual specifically chose to read further into a particular concept or ideology. This involved an active choice that one had to make. In contrast, the filter bubble makes the choices, and the user is in a more passive position. This means that users can be completely unaware of their presence within a filter bubble, as there is no moment at which the bubble is revealed to them; no moment at which they must actively put on the rose-coloured glasses. Rather, the rose-tinted filter was there all along, unbeknown to the user. Not only are these personal filter bubbles extremely difficult to avoid, but the process of which the user is not conscious also leads to isolation. In this way, the filter bubble serves as a new obstacle to overcoming Williams's notion of political tribalism. Thus, the new features of the digital space create new problems of an equal—if not greater—magnitude than the new opportunities they also create.

Filter bubbles have new and unique implications for political tribalism. They serve as a means of reinforcing users' existing views, whether or not that is the purpose of the bubbles. Williams notes that one of the keys to overcoming political tribalism is the cultivation of learning, especially by communicating and debating with those who hold different or opposing opinions. This learning allows one to undergo a complex process of adjustment to modify or challenge one's views, so that they are either strengthened or subjected to change as a result of the choices that the individual makes. The filter bubbles present in the digital world frustrate this process of learning, as they direct users into a dialogue with other members of their 'tribe' who share their sentiments. For learning to take place, one must be involved in discourse with those who share opposing views, so that one realises that there are ways of thinking about problems that are rational, even though they differ from one's own.

Filter bubbles not only hinder attempts to overcome political tribalism but also serve to strengthen it amongst individuals. Filter bubbles increase the separation between individuals with different opinions and bring closer together individuals with similar opinions. As such, they help create an environment that is increasingly tribalist. This is made possible by users' constant existence within a filter bubble that leads to a cultivation of confirmation bias and a passionate avoidance of anything that may cause some form of cognitive dissonance within the user. Extended exposure to only those who are like-minded will lead to an attitude of dismissiveness or aggression, with an inability to commune with anyone else who does not share a similar sentiment.

The bubbles also allow users to gain what they believe to be an intellectual superiority over others. When one's opinion is strengthened by the seemingly impartial media one consumes, it imbues one with an intellectual arrogance that cannot be gained through other methods. This arrogance is then exerted against other groups and users by dismissing their alternative opinions as false or fake. It is near impossible for learning to take place when one cannot recognise that other opinions are also rational and could hold some truth that one's own personal opinion is lacking. The filter bubbles breed a population that does not know how to converse charitably with those who are different from themselves, a population, in turn, which cannot cultivate an environment of learning. As such, filter bubbles create a new obstacle that must be overcome before the digital space can create an opportunity to learn and hence to overcome political tribalism.

Although filter bubbles do create a new and unique problem, this problem is not unsolvable. One can overcome their effects and enable the digital space to be utilised as a force that can conquer political tribalism. In its current form, the digital space is something that permits a culture of tribalism to grow due to the invisible, algorithmic, personalised editing of experiences within it. One option for overcoming these problems could be a restructuring of the digital space so that the algorithms are not developed in a way that causes division or isolation, but rather to provide a balance of opinions in the content shown to users. This change could mean that the digital space would be used to facilitate learning as envisaged by the idealistic view of the space. This learning could manifest in the form of being exposed to different opinions and ideas, leading a user to gain a wider and more holistic understanding of society. The user could then come to understand the significance and importance of others' opinions and how they can relate to and strengthen one's own, even though they are different. Undertaking this process may be difficult, however, as it could give rise to new filter bubbles. Rather than exposing users to a single opinion, modified algorithms might still only expose them to a select few. There is no way in which an algorithm that has a limited capacity can equally encompass every viewpoint. It also has implications for the individual who must make the decision as to where to strike the balance between the different opinions. The first page of Google can only be so long.

A much more effective method of transforming the digital space into something that could be utilised to overcome political tribalism could be a new form of learning: a learning defined by awareness. A solution could lie in educating individuals about the fact that what is seen in the digital space is not actually the whole picture. If it was clear that search results, news feeds, and advertisements were not all that they appear to be, users could have their agency restored as they would now be able to make the choice to search deeper, to connect with different people, and ultimately to have their ideas challenged. The digital space in its current form allows for these bubbles to remain invisible to the user. It is in the best interests of the user to become aware of their impacts, as the continuation of the naivete regarding the bubbles only allows for the problems to multiply in the future. Education about the presence of filter bubbles leads to an awareness of the bubbles, this awareness produces a restoration of agency for the user. When the filter bubbles are no longer invisible, and when their parameters are revealed, users know exactly where to push to escape from the isolation. If they can see the walls that isolate them, they can realise that they are in fact isolated, and can then endeavour to remedy the situation. Through this education, the digital space could become a force that assists in overcoming political tribalism. The digital space could then be used in line with its idealistic intentions and truly become a place of liberty and expression, and ultimately a place of learning.

The structure of digital space is unique. It permits issues to be over-amplified to the point at which they become significantly potent, so they require solutions that are of equal potency. Over-amplification frustrates efforts to overcome political tribalism. It occurs through filter bubbles that trap individuals in intellectual isolation. The filter bubbles create an environment that is increasingly tribal. This leads to aggression towards others, dismissal of alternative opinions, and the loss of individuals' ability to converse with others who hold different opinions. This renders the digital space harmful to social progress.

The digital space could be a valuable resource for overcoming political tribalism. There is no doubt that it will remain a ubiquitous feature of people's lives in future. So we must endeavour to work out how the digital space can become a resource for overcoming, rather than reinforcing, political tribalism. If not through the intensive restructuring of the digital space, perhaps what is required is education that enables people to be aware of the effect of the filter bubbles in which they operate, and so to restore their agency and allow people the ability to break free from the entrapment they bring.

9

DEFENDING THE 'I' IN TRIBE

SANDRA C. JONES

> Learning is a way of *telling the story of change* . . . we acknowledge that what *once* seemed adequate may be challenged; that moments of conflict and difficulty may be generative; that therefore our practices of knowing and understanding are about responding with tolerable success to what we don't control.
>
> Rowan Williams

The medical and social understanding of autism has a long history of conflict and difficulty. Autism research, policy, and public discourse is replete with divergent views on causation, diagnosis, presentation, representation, terminology, and treatment. History holds a number of disproven claims about 'causes', such as vaccinations and refrigerator mothers; and harmful 'treatments', such as chelation and drinking chlorine dioxide (bleach).[1] Autism Spectrum Disorder, as it is currently known, was first identified by the parallel reports of 'autism' by Austrian-American psychiatrist Leo Kanner in 1943 and 'little professors' by Austrian paediatrician Hans Asperger in 1944.[2] Although Kanner and Asperger both included classic behaviours of autism in their diagnostic criteria, Kanner considered those with 'autism' to be of average intelligence whilst Asperger considered 'little professors' to be highly intelligent. Autism, or Autism Spectrum Condition (ASC), is a neurodevelopmental condition that causes anatomical and functional differences in the brain, resulting in difficulties in social communication, repetitive behaviours, and restricted interests.[3]

Historically, autism was viewed through the lens of a medical model of disability, whereby an individual is perceived as having an inherent problem that limits their capabilities. In recent times, there has been a shift toward the social model of disability, reflecting changing attitudes within society, as the barriers faced by an individual are recognised as a result of their established environment. The socio-cultural shift toward an all-inclusive society has positioned autism as an example of the normal diversity of the human brain, rather than a deficit or disability.[4] The 'neurodiversity' movement is gaining momentum with those who identify as 'neurodiverse' describing the societal majority as 'neurotypical'. Whilst tensions between these two groups offer a broader contextual overview of the political landscape surrounding autism, this essay focuses on tribal divisions *within* the autism community.

The introduction of online tribes is a natural development, given that humans instinctively form tribes; we surround ourselves by people who look, act, and think like we do. Confirmation bias contends we pay more attention to voices and perspectives that resonate with our own,[5] and avoid the discomfort of cognitive dissonance by distancing ourselves from those whose viewpoints conflict with ours.[6] For many autistic people the internet provides a comfortable space, and a platform to speak from, protected from many of the challenges and complexities of face-to-face communication in a predominantly neurotypical society. While there are many positives of online platforms, including the ability to meet and connect with people, social media amplifies this natural tendency to form tribes with shared perspectives and life experiences. Algorithms fill our online feeds with content that aligns with our beliefs and interests. Over time, we increasingly overestimate the prevalence of our perspective and reduce our empathy for others:

> your filter bubble is your own personal, unique universe of information that you live in online. And what's in your filter bubble depends on who you are, and it depends on what you do. But the thing is that you don't decide what gets in. And more importantly, you don't actually see what gets edited out.[7]

Groupthink is the logical extension of being encased in a filter bubble, limiting our ability to think rationally and morally; "regarding those outside the group as enemies, censoring opposing ideas, and pressuring members to conform".[8] The capability to friend/like/join, unfriend/unlike/leave, mute and block individuals and groups creates an artificial world in which the majority share a language and an ethos— and the minority are silenced or isolated.

What's in a name like aspie or autistic? For those within the autism community, one of the most contentious and ongoing challenges is the adoption of words and phrases to identify the condition. This enduring debate reflects more than simple language preferences; reflecting deep communal divides, the forming and reforming of tribes, and continuing tribal politics. These divides run parallel to the changes in diagnostic criteria led by the medical community that have evolved over many decades, with the major changes outlined in Table 1 below. It is noteworthy that the disparate diagnoses of Asperger's Disorder and Autism introduced in 1994 (and removed in 2013) were in place for a period of nineteen years, the longest standing of any changes made to autism in the American Psychiatric Association's Diagnostic and Statistical Manual of Mental Disorders (DSM). This may contribute to the strong identities formed by individuals diagnosed during this period of time.

Table 1: Evolution of Autism Diagnostic Criteria

Year	Diagnostic Manual	Descriptions of Autism
1952	DSM-I	Schizophrenic Reaction, Childhood Type
1968	DSM-II	Schizophrenia, Childhood Type
1980	DSM-III	Infantile Autism
1987	DSM-IIIR	Autistic Disorder, including PDD-NOS
1994	DSM-IV	Asperger's Disorder, Autism Spectrum
2013	DSM-V	Autism Spectrum Disorder

The introduction of the DSM-V in 2013 was controversial for a number of reasons, not least due to its potential impact on the already established social identities of those diagnosed as 'Asperger's', who perceived themselves as 'Aspies'. There also existed a number of advocacy groups (e.g. Aspergers Victoria, Aspie Rebels), academic journals and books (e.g. *Aspergirls* by Rudy Simone, *The Complete Guide to Asperger's Syndrome* by Tony Attwood), websites, and social media groups. However, some within the autism community, aspies and autistics alike, found the distinction divisive and ableist; presupposing that aspies saw themselves as 'better' or 'less disabled' than autistics. This is a battle that rages fiercely on social media platforms, with many online autism groups banning the terms 'Asperger's' or 'Aspie' either implicitly, through criticism of posts, or explicitly, through their online group rules. One Facebook post that expresses frustration about this situation reads:

> Why are people policing adjectives in every single Facebook group about autism? Autist, Aspie, Aspergian . . . ??? . . . please leave me and my identity that I am comfortable with alone please.

Do the language and labels we use to describe a person or an identity matter? There has been continuing debate in the academic literature and in public discourse around the use of person-first versus identity-first language.[9] Person-first language (e.g. 'a person with autism') is argued by its proponents to position the disability as one of several features of the individual rather than as a primary defining characteristic. Identity-first language (e.g. 'an autistic person') is argued by its proponents to acknowledge that the disability is an integral part of the individual, intertwined with their identity; it is not something we acquire and lose, or pick up and put down. There is also the related issue of the connotative meaning of these distinctions; and the human tendency to claim and internalise positive traits and outcomes while distancing or externalising negative traits and outcomes. This is perhaps best exemplified in the tradition in the academic literature to refer to 'children with autism' and 'typically developing children'; the former separates the 'negative' (autism) from the child's identity, whereas the latter connects the 'positive' (typical development) to the child's identity. The dilemma is captured in the observation that "If you think it is bad to say I am autistic, it means you think it is bad to be autistic".[10]

Another area of contention among the autism community is the labels used to describe autistic people based on their level of function, i.e. high functioning or low functioning. Those who support these labels see them as providing a useful distinction in determining the level of support that may be required for the individual. Those who oppose the labels see them as offensive and misleading, e.g. 'high-functioning' underestimates the challenges people face and 'low-functioning' underestimates the strengths people have.[11] Underlying the choice of terminology is a perceived multi-layered debate about the meaning, aetiology, diagnosis, acceptance, and treatment of autism. These debates result in the formation of tribes, where social media provides a fertile platform for strong intra-tribal identification and animosity.

The most contentious battlefront in the autistic community (both online and offline) is that between 'adult autistics' and parents of 'children with autism'; a dispute which is highlighted by the preference for identity-first language among the former and for person-first language among the latter.

From the introduction of autism as a diagnostic category, the focus has been on the identification and diagnosis of children—positioning parents as the primary advocates and spokespeople for autistic children. Many of these parents have had to fight arduous battles to obtain diagnoses and support for their children, to enable them to attend and participate in education, and to challenge stigma and discrimination. However, as the first generations of *diagnosed* autistic people entered adulthood, we began to hear the voices of autistic adults, advocating for themselves and for other autistic people. These voices are particularly strident among those who were diagnosed as adults; people who spent their childhood and adolescence misunderstood, misdiagnosed, and marginalised.

The autism rights activist, Jim Sinclair, is widely credited with steering the conversation away from the needs and expectations of parents and towards those of their children in his 1993 essay, "Don't Mourn for Us", which calls to parents: "Grieve if you must, for your own lost dreams. But don't mourn for us. We are alive. We are real. And we're here waiting for you".[12]

Almost twenty years later, armed with a clear autistic identity and unprecedented opportunities to reach large audiences via social media, autistic people are claiming their right to speak about their experiences and to speak on behalf of those who do not have the capacity or opportunity to do so. Facebook (and other social media platforms) host a wide range of groups and pages that bring together autistic people to share their experiences and advocate for societal change.

A historical lens on autism shows us that these generational perspectives are, in part, a by-product of the growing and changing understanding of the autistic condition. Williams notes that tribalism marks out certain (non-modern) kinds of human behaviour as *aberrations from the norm*:

> What's more, it is—again, naturally enough—seen as imperfectly human, so that life lived within these terms is less than it should be, less than the fullness that we now enjoy and have grown into. Non-modern life is a *deprived* life, so that the efforts to eradicate it can be seen as part of a struggle for fullness of human experience . . .

For the earlier generations of autistic people, autism was seen as an imperfectly human condition that needed to be cured—and many experienced harsh and harmful 'treatments' at the hands of (generally well-intentioned) parents and health professionals. As our understanding of autism has expanded, including our recognition of the strengths of autistic people and the fullness of their experiences, we have moved to recognition of the need to modify attitudes and environments to be more supportive and inclusive. For the former, autism was the scourge to be eradicated; for the latter, those who seek to 'cure' or 'treat' autism at great cost to the autistic person are the scourge to be eradicated.

Thus, while we have two groups of people with a passionate desire to address the same predicament, they have different perspectives on what the problems are that lead to the predicament, and thus different (and often conflicting) views on how it can be solved. The mutually agreed predicament is, essentially, "how can autistic people flourish in a world dominated by neurotypical people?" For many parents (and health practitioners) the 'problems' that lead to this predicament are intrinsic to the autism diagnosis; and the solutions are curing or treating the autistic person so that they become (or appear) more like neurotypical people. Thus, their child will (in their eyes) be able to live a full and complete life. Conversely, for many autistic adults the 'problems' that lead to this predicament are intrinsic to the social and physical environment; and the solutions are modifying the environments to make it more appropriate, accessible, and welcoming for autistic people so that they can live full and complete *autistic* lives.

As Williams eloquently notes, "Political tribalism is above all a shrinkage of the scope of mutual recognition: I resolve not to think of the other's view as sharing any of the moral anxieties or emotional tensions I experience". In reality, both 'tribes' share a commitment to achieving the best possible outcomes for autistic children, but their perspectives on what these outcomes are and how to achieve them are often very different. Parents may feel a sense of grief and loss upon receiving their child's diagnosis, as they grapple with the thought that their child's future may not be as they imagined it; autistic adults may find this response hurtful and discriminatory, as they do not see their autistic identity as less desirable than neurotypical identity. Parents may also struggle with the challenges of bringing up an autistic child in a neurotypical society (even more so if they themselves are neurotypical and have limited understanding of autism); autistic adults may reflect on their childhood and the experience of being made to feel like a burden on their family.

Parents may search for a treatment or a cure for their child's autism as they perceive that this will give them a better life; autistic adults may see this as an offensive and harmful suggestion that autistic people are damaged and need to be 'fixed' to be valuable members of society. These are more than philosophical debates as some of the 'treatments' that have been proposed for autism are physically harmful—in addition to the potential psychological harm of autistic children growing up feeling that they are damaged or inadequate.

Many autistic adults (of the current generation) lived through childhoods in which their autism was defined as an illness to be cured; they endured distressing and sometimes harmful 'treatments' aimed at making them behave like neurotypical children and forcing them to mask their true selves at great physical and emotional cost. Others were undiagnosed in childhood but categorised as 'odd' or 'difficult' and grew up feeling flawed and ashamed of who they are as people.

Autistic advocates may also differ in the nature and extent to which their autism impacts on their daily lives. While it is important to avoid the use of functioning labels, and to recognise that all autistic people experience challenges living in a neurotypical world, we must also recognise that parents are often advocating for children with very high support needs and limited tools for communication. We must also recognise that parents are people; while we can aspire to a world where autistic people (and all people) are loved and accepted as they are, the reality of caring for a child—or indeed an adult—with very high support needs can be exhausting. An autistic adult may (rightly) feel challenged and offended by hearing a parent speak of their child as a burden; but a parent may (rightly) feel challenged and offended by being accused of not loving their child when they are genuinely exhausted from the strain of providing full-time care to a child (or adult) with challenging behaviours, as is expressed in the following Facebook post:

> my son is 6 and has recently started hitting his head on objects. usually I can counter with my hand or a pillow but now it's to the point it's on corners and hard enough to leave marks and he laughs and says again . . .

This has resulted in an environment where autistic adults challenge parents, saying, "You can't speak for your child, because you aren't autistic"; and parents challenge autistics, saying, "You can't speak for my child because your autism is not like their autism." As with any tribal issue, neither group is entirely correct. There is certainly an argument to be made that a neurotypical parent may never really understand how it feels to be autistic in the same way that another autistic can and continue to interpret their child's emotions and behaviours from a neurotypical lens (for example, they might understand intellectually that their child is hyper-sensitive to light, but not understand physiologically the level of pain or discomfort that entails). Equally, there is an argument to be made that an autistic person cannot speak for another autistic person who has a different profile of strengths and challenges, particularly one they have never met, whereas a parent who spends every day with that child will have an insight into their life and reactions. As the autistic academic and speaker, Stephen Shore, puts it, "If you've met one person with autism, you've met one person with autism."

Social media serves as both a magnifier and a spiral for these differences. Many parents of autistic children belong to parent groups, established by other parents, which they join to learn more about autism and parenting an autistic child. Again, these groups provide an important platform for sharing of experiences, challenges, supports, and successes—but they often focus on challenges and disappointments, magnified by reading of others' parenting challenges, in an environment where the voices of autistic people and the stories of their successes and talents are increasingly absent. In these groups, parents are often considered 'martyrs', suffering through the experience of raising an autistic child and/or 'warriors' fighting for their children. However, as the following Facebook posts demonstrate, by positioning parents of autistic children as martyrs and warriors, they (inadvertently or otherwise) position autistic people as a burden:

> "Every mother who raises an autistic child is the best mother in the world"
>
> "Trying to get her to focus on school work is impossible. And don't look at her wrong or she may cry or have a meltdown!!! I need a drink . . . and I don't even drink"

Many autistic adults belong to Facebook groups that have written or unwritten rules that only autistic people can join or (while others can join) only autistic people can comment. While these groups provide an important platform for sharing of experiences, challenges, supports, and successes they can also provide a platform for hard criticism of parents of autistic children. For many, this stems from childhood trauma and mistreatment, magnified by reading of others' childhood trauma and mistreatment, and spiralling as the voices of those with supportive parents are silent and the voices of parents are absent.

As noted above, these diverse groups largely share common goals: building a society that is accepting of autistic differences and maximising opportunities for autistic people to achieve their potential (and particularly their potential to feel included and accepted). However, current communication channels serve to maximise the differences and minimise the similarities. Facebook and Google algorithms mean that people learning about their (or their child's) autism can be sucked into a vortex where they are increasingly exposed to one perspective and are not exposed to, or given the opportunity to engage in, healthy discussions about different perspectives and needs. Facebook groups which set strong rules around terminology (with the genuine intention of protecting, supporting, and empowering their targeted membership) also serve to silence other voices and reduce the capacity to share diverse perspectives and educate others. These two features of electronic communication make it difficult to ask questions, to share diverse experiences, and—most importantly—to come together to advocate for the societal and environmental changes that would benefit all autistic people.

This is amplified for autistic people, whose neurotype means that they tend to comply with rules and routines, and often have difficulty seeing another person's perspective or understanding that other people have unique thoughts, ideas, and personal motivations. Autistic people (and particularly those who are newly diagnosed) can find themselves challenged in groups for their expressions of concern about their diagnosis, and accused of ableism. This can result in them feeling more isolated and confused and unsupported by their 'tribe', as expressed, for instance, in this Facebook post:

> 'aspie supremacists' think they're better than other autistics because they're 'high functioning' . . .

Parents who join groups of other parents are often exposed predominantly to the challenges, rather than the potential, of the autistic experience. They are encouraged to see their children as burdens and themselves as warriors; with the effect of negating the voices of autistic people. For example, one Facebook post reads,

> It's so hard some days to look at him and wonder what his life would be like if he was smarter and 'normal' so to speak. You know get good grades and have friends . . .

However, those who join groups of autistic people can find themselves challenged and criticised for their choice of language, their expression of challenges, or their seeking of support and reassurance, as demonstrated by this Facebook post:

> Have you ever been on 'autism moms' pages? They never listen to autistics, they make everything about themselves and play the victims.

As Williams notes, "What happens when we forget how to tell our story in this way? We come to resist any notion that what we take for granted as settled is not instantly self-evident, and we lose the sense that engagement with the alien and the unplanned is a potential source of insight and enrichment."

The tendency for people to hold strongly to their own views, and to find it difficult to recognise the validity of other perspectives, is perhaps amplified in the autism community. While the claim that autistic people lack theory of mind has increasingly been discredited,[13] it is generally acknowledged that autistic people hold strong attitudes, have difficulties with expressive communication and social interaction, and may be resistant to change. For example, the above-mentioned discomfort with the changes to the DSM-V which served for many to invalidate the strongly held identity inherent in the label. Further complicating the potential for conflict between autistic adults and parents of autistic children is the possibility that many of these parents may themselves be undiagnosed autistics who are unaware of their own communication challenges.

There is a need for healthy, open, and sensitive inter-tribal discussion that recognises and values people's different perspectives and experiences. Williams reminds us of the importance of a shared language in facilitating ongoing and constructive dialogue—polarised language fuels polarised debate. As outlined above, the tribal languages in this context are embedded with words of deep connotative meaning. To many of those diagnosed under DSM-IV, 'Asperger's' is both a diagnostic label and an identity, for others it is separatist and elitist.[14] To many parents, 'child with autism' is the terminology of clinical interactions as well as a function of the process of adjusting to their child's diagnosis; to many autistic adults, it is a denial of the child's identity and a rejection of their uniqueness.

Williams makes the powerful point that overcoming political tribalism requires more than civility and empathy; it needs respectful debate that acknowledges that both tribes seek to resolve the same predicament. However, each has a different conceptualisation of the predicament and a different view of the problems to be solved to achieve this resolution. Both groups need to be willing to recognise the validity of each other's perspectives; and to seek solutions to both sets of problems.

Social media brings both opportunities and challenges into this space. In many ways, it has been social media that has enabled the voices of autistic people to be heard (by each other, by families, and by the broader community). Similarly, it has been social media, and the internet more broadly, that has provided parents with unprecedented access to information and resources to support their autistic children.

Conversely, social media has played a large part in the formation of tribes and the escalation of conflict, enabling people to form communities of intensely shared perspectives, where diverging views are absent or silenced. As Williams explains:

> The more a moral or social position is taken to be timelessly self-evident in this way, the more moral reproach is attached to any doubt or denial of it—and so the less room remains for any attempt at finding a common language for debate and shared reflection. This particular aspect of political discourse is currently one of the major challenges to the future of democracy. A political debate in which your opponent is not merely mistaken, unwise, or uninformed, but malignant and/or sub-rational, is one in which (say) the winner and the loser in an election have no stake in accommodating one another . . .

Parents of autistic children need to recognise that autistic adults have a lot to bring to the conversation, including a deep understanding of how it feels to be autistic and how families and carers can nurture their children's strengths and support them to become confident and fulfilled adults. They need to understand that for autistic adults the problems to be solved include stigma, isolation, exclusion, and a range of environmental and social barriers to living an authentically autistic life. At the same time, autistic adults need to recognise that parents bring a deep personal understanding of their own autistic child, and that there are genuine challenges for parents which require us to provide support rather than criticism. They need to understand that for parents the problems to be solved include keeping their child safe, balancing the child's needs with those of other family members, and dealing with the logistical and emotional challenges of bringing up a child whose thoughts and behaviours are fundamentally different from their own.

If we are to build a society that accepts and supports autistic people, there is a lot of work to be done in educating schools, communities, governments, and other agencies. We need to recognise that both sets of problems are real and valid, and that together we can develop solutions that begin to address both sets of problems. The energy that is invested in these inter-tribal conflicts could be channelled into advocating for better outcomes for all autistic people.

All of the tribes discussed above have a shared goal—better outcomes for autistic people. This is, as Williams describes it, a *shared social territory*. There is a need for respectful discussion to map out this territory and determine how our diverse perspectives can be brought together around common moral values and shared goals. Only when the various tribes understand, and respect, each other's perspectives—and are prepared to make compromises to find the kernel of a shared understanding of the problems—can they come together as a powerful voice to advocate for the social and environmental changes needed to create a more inclusive and accepting world for autistic children and adults alike.

10

SUSTAINING SOCIETY

ANNETTE PIERDZIWOL

How can we "salvage an intelligent, compassionate and pluralist democracy from the wreckage of so much contemporary political habit"? Part of the answer proposed by Rowan Williams in his lecture is to claim that we must give renewed attention to what makes for a *sustainable* political democracy. In the face of deep and harmful political divides, we need a better understanding of what sustains the life of a society, and thus of the work that can be done to preserve society through moments of significant challenge, disagreement, and change. As Williams argues, part of pushing back against political tribalism "means accepting that the other, even the opponent, has a continuing presence and stake in a shared social territory so that the task becomes one of *finding what sustains that shared territory* and defends us from zero-sum violence in our conflicts." To do so, we must find the key stabilising ingredient; as Williams puts it, we must find the "most significant preservative for law-governed democracy in contemporary societies." What could perform this role? What preservative will allow us to sustain an intelligent, compassionate, and pluralist democracy?

In this essay, I explore Williams's answer to this question, which in large part focuses on having the time and putting in the effortful labour needed for attentive narrative exchange across different views and negotiating shared paths forward. To help elucidate Williams's account, I compare it with a somewhat different proposal from the American political philosopher, Martha C. Nussbaum. The comparison is illuminating since I take it that both writers are moved by essentially the same problem—the problem of ensuring the stability and motivational sustainability of liberal democratic societies—yet both develop their answers differently. The comparison is also illuminating since Nussbaum and Williams tend to work in very different intellectual traditions: Williams draws on Christian political theology and Nussbaum draws on—and, indeed, seeks to improve and extend—Rawlsian liberalism. However, as I'll show, their answers are only partially different; there is an interesting commonality between Williams's and Nussbaum's view about the most powerful force for sustaining society. I examine how Nussbaum frames this issue of stability as a "problem in the history of liberalism" and answers it by appealing to emotion and particularly to love. I then explore how her appeal to love can complement Williams's account, as well as drawing in an insight from the Scottish Enlightenment philosopher, David Hume, that dovetails with and enriches both accounts.

One key to understanding Williams's proposal is to appreciate that it operates on the terrain of practical wisdom. He argues that the key to sustaining the shared life of a society, and any shared future for it, will be to focus on finding "manageable solutions to specific unjust situations", or "sustainable solutions to particular challenges or inequities", or again "solutions that have a degree of durability and credibility, even if they are no-one's ideal". What is needed, he argues, is a form of public moral discernment and decision-making done at this practical level: "*clarifying* problems, identifying claims as clearly as possible, and looking for a sustainable way forward". Citizens seeking to foster a sustainable political democracy will thus need to train their attention onto the particular, becoming adept at analysing practical problems and at devising solutions that work for their particular context.[1] For Williams, both of these tasks can only be achieved by coming together across different groups and interests. First, with regard to clarifying practical problems, one must attend to the particular narratives of those persons they concern. Secondly, with regard to devising solutions, one must "work together at what a manageable (sustainable) future might look like" for all concerned, negotiating what courses of action and social arrangements might constitute a way of going on together that could be sustained over time.

Williams highlights that this "negotiated problem-solving" across social divides will necessarily involve compromise. Especially where serious conflicts of power are at stake, there will be "the inevitabilities of loss and cost in the processes of negotiating a shared future." No one group will end up with the embodiment of their pre-determined ideal. Nor is the aim to find a shared ideal—an ideal core held in common between different comprehensive moral views. As Williams explains, what he means by searching for shared languages certainly doesn't "necessitate shared views", instead, by this he has in mind something that would "enable a more protracted engagement on issues"; a basis for moral discourse and disagreement. For example, he talks about this as an attempt "to discover what the 'grammar' of another's moral energy has in common with my own, *as the condition for intelligent action.*" It is important to note, then, that for Williams this striving to find something humanly recognisable and morally intelligible in another's views doesn't in any way mean compromising one's own moral views:

> To be clear: this is not a bland appeal for civility in political debate. That would too easily be reduced to an appeal not to be so emotionally invested in our beliefs, which is a futile recommendation. It is an appeal for some kind of work to grasp the history and structure of the 'investment' of the stranger.

For Williams, it is only through the work of listening and negotiated problem-solving that new possibilities can be opened up. As different groups and interests work together to determine a course of action that could be lived in a sustainable way for each of them, previously unforeseen strategies and pathways can emerge. Indeed, it is the pre-emptive closing off of new possibilities that comprises Williams's key complaint with political tribalism in the lecture:

> The deepest problem with political tribalism, the all-or-nothing rhetoric of the electoral politics of the United States or the Brexit debates nearer home, is that it turns its back on *the possibility of horizons expanding*—even where fundamental orientations don't change radically. And conversely, the major challenge of moving beyond such tribalism, with its scapegoating and demonizing and lack of collective self-scrutiny, is the building of a culture that is confident, trustful enough to give time for perspectives to interact and interrogate one another and themselves. Building such a culture is intrinsic to building something more than a 'strong' state or nation—the creation of *durable* human solidarity, within and between states.

This then seems to be a central plank of Williams's account of what sustains a society: it is the interaction and interrogation of perspectives, through processes of listening and negotiation—processes which he emphasises multiple times will require prolonged time and labour. They involve an effort of the understanding. But they also involve, as I'll explore shortly, emotional efforts to rehearse and imaginatively inhabit the emotional investment the other has in their moral convictions and the way these provide an intelligible ground and motivation for their actions.

I turn now to Martha Nussbaum's proposal about how to sustain a decent and stable society over time. Nussbaum's account both intersects with and illuminates certain aspects of Williams's account in valuable ways.

In her 2013 book, *Political Emotions: Why Love Matters for Justice*, Nussbaum argues that there is a "problem in the history of liberalism" from Locke onwards in that it has failed to adequately address one of its own essential criteria. Namely, as Nussbaum explains, "part of justifying a normative political project is showing that it can be reasonably stable",[2] or again "showing that the just society can be stable is a necessary part of its justification".[3] The key challenge Nussbaum issues on this front, however, is to insist that achieving stability "requires grappling with the complexities of real human psychology;"[4] the particularistic bent of the human mind, and "the quirky ways in which real people are moved".[5] It means recognising the unavoidable power of emotion in human life and the ways it can undermine the stability of a society, for example, through narrowness of sympathy or darker emotions such as disgust and envy that lead us to dehumanise others. For Nussbaum, liberal political philosophers have ignored the emotional terrain at their peril, especially given their task all along has been to show that the just society can be sustained—and this by real human beings. But even more so, as anti-liberal forces have had no qualms recognising its importance and making use of strong public emotion to secure stability and motivational force for their visions for society. For Nussbaum, then, emotion is integral to the task of showing how liberal democratic societies can be reasonably stable.

Motivated by this focus on emotion as a potential force to sustain society, Nussbaum is particularly interested in discovering forms of political or "public emotion that can themselves be stable over time" and thus help provide psychological support for just institutions and laws.[6] She acknowledges that "great democratic leaders, in many times and places, have understood the importance of cultivating appropriate emotions (and discouraging those that obstruct society's progress towards its goals)" and her book seeks to learn from a number of examples, such as Abraham Lincoln, Martin Luther King Jr, Mahatma Gandhi, and Jawaharlal Nehru. Nussbaum laments that "liberal political philosophy, however, has, on the whole, said little about the topic".[7] Her aim in *Political Emotions* is to provide this supplement for political liberalism by developing an account of the "psychology of the decent society" and "a blueprint for the cultivation of strong sustaining emotions" that can support it.[8]

The kernel of Nussbaum's argument, summed up in the subtitle of the book, is to show "why love matters for justice". She writes: "I shall argue that all of the core emotions that sustain a decent society have their roots in, or are forms of, love—by which I mean intense attachments to things outside the control of our will".[9] One of the most interesting elements of the book's argument is this emphasis on intense attachments or particularised loves and the vital role they play in human motivation and action. This is what Nussbaum labels the "eudaimonistic thought" and it is a claim she returns to at a number of key junctures in the argument:

> all the major emotions are "eudaimonistic," meaning they appraise the world from the person's own viewpoint and the viewpoint, therefore, of that person's evolving conception of a worthwhile life. We grieve for people we care about, not for total strangers. We fear damages that threaten ourselves and those we care about, not earthquakes on Mars. Eudaimonism is not egoism: we may hold that other people have intrinsic value. But the ones who will stir a deep emotion in us are the ones to whom we are somehow connected through our imagining of a valuable life, what I shall henceforth call our "circle of concern".[10]

For Nussbaum, drawing upon the strong emotions and motives which are a natural feature of human beings' partiality is key to any attempt to stabilise the just society. Rather than attempting to eradicate, or in some way correct, the strong partial concern human beings tend to feel towards those in their immediate circle—"our erotic investment in the world, our attachments to our own team, our own love, our own children, our own life"[11]—Nussbaum argues we need to expand it. In particular, drawing on the work of social psychologist C. Daniel Batson, she argues that we should focus on the powerful psychological tendency people have to feel compassion for the suffering of those they love and strong accompanying motivation to help them when in need, even if this involves great sacrifice.[12] For Nussbaum, extending and channelling this emotion into the political realm is vital for sustaining society. But we will only be able to do so if we remember its 'eudaimonistic' nature. To return to the topic of Williams's lecture, this means that if people across deep political divides "are to get a grip on our emotions", according to Nussbaum, "these emotions must somehow position them within our circle of concern, creating a sense of 'our' life in which these people and events matter as parts of our 'us,' our own flourishing."[13]

But how does this movement take place—how can another person with whom I deeply disagree come to matter in my scheme of things such that we might see ourselves as having the kind of shared future Williams discusses? Nussbaum would argue that we can attempt to intentionally extend this circle through "indirect appeals to the emotions" by using narrative infused with imagery, symbolism, memory, poetry, and so on.[14] She suggests that narrative—especially vivid portrayals, well-crafted rhetoric and artworks that seek to "inspire deliberately strong emotion"—can have a motivational and stabilising power that abstract principles rarely approach.[15] Of course, as she notes, "any complete discussion would need to be fortified with lots of data, since a story might paint a distorted picture" but, she argues, "the story, unlike the data, powerfully brings its reader close" to the life of the other, "making her part of their 'eudaimonistic' circle of concern in a way that a more detached description could not".[16] Such narratives, drawing on the vivid particulars of a place, history, symbol, and so on, can inspire emotions and motives (such as compassion in response to others' pain and altruistic motivation to help), which link people together as an 'us' and wherein others gradually become part of one's practical deliberations about possible courses of action and the contours of a sustainable future.

Nussbaum's view on the emotional force of narrative adds a further dimension to Williams's emphasis on narrative listening by suggesting another possible approach for those keen to take a leadership role in pursuing the "labour of cultural change". Their role could involve not just "looking for or constructing contexts in which narrative sharing is possible" via opening up spaces within society for those citizens who are willing and able to engage in this extended listening. It might also involve attempts to construct or facilitate the construction of narratives in the form of various cultural artefacts that vividly engage imagination and emotion. In so doing, they would be 'working with the grain' of the particularistic bent of human psychology and providing another—perhaps broader—road for those lacking the time or inclination to engage in the prolonged labour of attentive listening that Williams outlines.

Indeed, there is further overlap here given the emphasis Williams places on the role of emotion in how we arrive at our deeply held views and how we should approach the task of listening and recognising the views of others. Central to this task on his account, as noted above, is to see the other's view as being as emotionally invested as my own. And so to try, as it were, to imaginatively recreate in a kind of hermeneutic of charity the journey of thought and feeling that may have led them to their convictions, seeing those views as being held with the same kind of investment and tensions with which we usually take our own to be held. This labour may once again provide vivid emotional fodder that could be translated into narrative and communicated to others. Of course, ideally, Williams would prefer all citizens to engage in this labour of emotional recognition, each training themselves in the capacity for it. But for some of the time-poor and attention-poor denizens of contemporary liberal democracies, having aspects of this work and its emotional journey vividly presented to them might be one way of inspiring further efforts of this sort. By helping kickstart feelings of care and concern through engaging imagination and emotion, vivid narrative presentations could prompt more deliberate efforts of the sort Williams outlines. Moreover, given, as Nussbaum highlights, that the salience produced by vivid depiction is often only temporary and easily reverts back to a smaller circle of concern, it is even more important that it gives rise to the more deliberate and sustained efforts Williams commends.

As we've seen, then, for Nussbaum, "the vivid presentation of another person's plight"—even of complete strangers or diametrically opposed political enemies—can, through the indirect appeal to strong emotions, such as compassion, serve to move "that person, temporarily, into the centre of the things that matter," bringing them into my circle of concern and helping open up questions about shared courses of action for 'our' mutual flourishing. Yet, given, as noted, this effect is typically only short-lived, it cannot alone answer the stability question that has been our focus. The challenge will be to find ways to extend the circle of concern to more people in ways that are stable and sustainable.

Nussbaum and Williams's views about the political importance of narrative and emotion can be enriched by considering the work of another thinker in the history of philosophy who was preoccupied with the role of the passions in social life, namely, David Hume. Another angle on approaching the challenge of extending our circle of concern, somewhat different from the vivid depiction route, can be found in what Hume calls the phenomenon of 'acquaintance' and his attention to the role habit can play in making us come to care even for 'strangers'. In the *Treatise of Human Nature*, Hume points to the way we contract "a habitude and intimacy" with a person by "frequenting his company".[17] And he contends that this phenomenon of acquaintance has "the same effect" and "operates in the same manner" as relations of blood—both have the effect of making a person matter to us and giving us a more lively sympathy with their passions.[18] Interestingly, Hume argues that what blood relations and acquaintances have in common is that they both give rise to love and affection:

> Whoever is united to us by any connection is always sure of a share of our love, proportioned to the connection . . . Thus the relation of blood produces the strongest tie the mind is capable of in the love of parents to their children, and a lesser degree of the same affection, as the relation lessens . . . There is another phenomenon, which is parallel to this, *viz.* that *acquaintance*, without any kind of relation, gives rise to love and kindness.[19]

If Hume is right that there is something like a phenomenon of habitual acquaintance that operates in a manner 'parallel' to blood relations to generate bonds of affection and attachment—and some contemporary psychological evidence appears to support this claim[20]—then perhaps the path of regular, embodied interaction might turn out to be one of the easier ways to work 'with the grain' of human psychology to stably extend our circles of concern.

Furthermore, it seems plausible that this is part of the reason why the "local and voluntary networks of affiliation" and "projects of community organising" that Williams discusses are so crucial. It is not only that they can open up excellent contexts for "unpressured listening to the narratives of neighbour and stranger", but also that they can sometimes succeed in turning those strangers into acquaintances; creating bonds of affection that bring them into one's circle of concern in such a way that they come to really matter to one. Interestingly, this means that even when the time and intentional effort for Williams's "patient attention" may be lacking, there are available indirect means, tapping into the tendencies of human psychology, that can be used to help extend our circle of concern—even across deep difference. The political rivals whose children attend the same school, or, in Williams's example, who sing in the same choir together, may devote precious little time at either activity to listening to one another's stories in the manner Williams commends. Yet, through the lived proximity of these experiences, they may still find themselves—almost despite themselves—attached to one another and factoring each other into their practical deliberations about a sustainable future.

It can be tempting to assume that such attachments and affection can never really be formed for those whose views are fundamentally opposed to our own. Indeed, it has been something of an ongoing feature of work on sympathy and love to suggest that it can only track those who are similar to us, though this is being questioned in some recent psychological studies.[21] The Berkley psychologist Alison Gopnik, who also happens to share an interest in the work of Hume, highlights another approach to our attachment relations (or, in Nussbaum's phrasing, our particularised loves) that she finds in the work of the economist, Robert Frank, and the philosopher, Kim Sterelny. According to Gopnik, they argue that

> the feelings that go with attachment—such as love, trust, and loyalty—allow people who have different capacities and clashing short-term interests to cooperate in a way that benefits everyone in the long run. Parents versus children, wives versus husbands, hunters versus gatherers—all of these relationships inevitably involve tension and conflict. Rationality and contractual negotiation alone can't resolve the differences that arise . . . But emotions can help. Sterelny argues that attachments act as

> "commitment mechanisms." They ensure that partners won't just walk out of an argument or renege on an agreement when it becomes inconvenient.[22]

The worry about contractual negotiation here resonates with Williams's claim that looking to "prescriptive or protective legislation" alone to guarantee certain rights won't be enough for sustaining cultural change in a way that doesn't risk pulling apart the social fabric. Rather, what's needed is something deeper, which, as he puts it, "has to do with the work of constructing a *culture* that is capable of containing disagreement and managing change in ways that do not violently disrupt the life of a society." That work, as Nussbaum highlights, will need to draw on emotion and in particular on love, pushing directly against what Williams labels "the wreckage of so much contemporary political habit" with its ever-present tendency to foster contempt for political rivals. It will need to extend the kind of love, commitment, and trust that defines our close relations towards those farther afield and even opposed to us.[22] The strategies surveyed in this essay from Williams, Nussbaum, and Hume provide insights into some of the emotional and motivational resources of human psychology which citizens might tap to provide a "preservative" for contemporary democratic societies and ensure their stability over time. In particular, it has been suggested that it is those deeper background feelings of concern and love that will enable a society to contain within itself passionate disagreement while at the same time remaining passionately and practically committed to a shared future.[24]

11

Two concepts of legitimacy

M. A. Casey

Much discussion of political tribalism gives the impression that it emerged fully formed from nowhere in 2016. While there are few who would claim that all was going swimmingly before the Brexit referendum and the American presidential election of that year, the extraordinary reaction to both events from the commanding heights of culture and politics conveyed a strong sense that History had been derailed. It was as if civility in political discourse, media as an impartial source of reliable information, deference to expert opinion, trust in beloved institutions, and positive engagement in the political process were all abruptly brought to an end with the outcomes of two unrelated democratic ballots. More considered enquiries have, of course, begun to trace out what happened along a much longer stretch of track, so that we can begin to understand what occurred in 2016 as less a rupture and more a fulfilment of a range of developments we have been happy to let run unchecked for a long time. Despite this growth in understanding, a fixture for much public discussion remains that some tribalism is primarily a problem arising from one side of the political spectrum, betokening a range of evils up to and including fascism; while the other side is assumed to be above tribalism and immune to the attractions of extremism.

Against this background, Lord Williams's discussion of political tribalism revolves around an unexpected example. His examination of Enlightenment tribalism situates the problem in a much longer time frame than the last fifty years, and looks beyond developments in politics, culture, and society to some of the intellectual presuppositions and habits of thought which modernity owes to Enlightenment thinking. These presuppositions have not only shaped ideas of knowledge and learning in the West, but also how engagement with difference is approached and understood. Enlightenment tribalism has given modernity its "default setting", a vision of what it means to be human that "does not really see itself as a culture among others" but as "a rational norm for fully flourishing human existence" that is universally valid. This default—"Westernising, 'technocratic', rights-oriented, and committed to individual autonomy as an ideal"—"entails a sharply exclusionary rhetoric about what is not standard modern practice, even when the human rights culture of the day mandates some sort of tolerance for non-standard communities". The exclusion of ways of life and thinking which do not conform to the modern default is not simply a function of imperialism. More importantly, it springs from a conviction that "non-modern life is a deprived life". It is "seen as imperfectly human, so that life lived within these terms is less than it should be, less than the fullness that we now enjoy and have grown into".

Williams nowhere uses the word 'elite' in his PM Glynn Lecture, but in many respects his account of Enlightenment tribalism describes the political tribalism of those who shape the regnant political, social, and cultural values in democratic societies, and who are often described or disparaged by this word. There are obviously also other forms of tribalism which do not share the Enlightenment universalism of the elite or its sense of the end of history, with all other ways of life and beliefs destined to disappear or converge within it. Some of these other tribalisms have developed directly in opposition to Enlightenment tribalism, often because of how it threatens ways of life and attachments to place which are important to people, but which it regards as aberrations from the norms of globalisation and efficiency, doomed in any case to extinction. The desire to preserve important attachments to the local, the particular, and even the national, need not lead to tribalism (it may simply be a form of resistance to economic changes, or a defence of communities) any more than a commitment to Enlightenment rationalism, when it is seen "as another set of learned perspectives rather than a timeless and self-evident system". Nor does tribalism necessarily entail political extremism on one side or the other, although political extremists on both sides are also malignly tribal. What the opponent tribalisms draw on and highlight, however, is the role that emotions play, particularly those such as fear of losing something important; the feeling that agency is diminished, that it is not possible to affect the remote and impersonal forces that are eroding a way of life; feeling disparaged for your beliefs, manners, customs, or habits; and not being taken seriously, not being recognised or treated as if you matter.

Enlightenment tribalism and its opponent tribalisms, while very different in content, nevertheless have some similar attributes. The members of these tribes see each other as imperfectly human and themselves as more completely human. They refuse recognition of the other, seeing the opponent as irredeemably alien, with whom it is not possible to converse or agree about anything important. The "moral anxieties or emotional tensions" that each group experiences are not shared, or understood as shareable, and to the extent that fear or anxiety is acknowledged as an important factor in opponent tribalism, Enlightenment tribalism treats it as a matter for reproach and as confirmation of the illegitimacy of the particular claims it advances. Williams notes the danger of "majoritarian tyranny" when it comes to how the outcomes and mandates of elections or referenda are described, and the Brexit result and the Trump election are sometimes offered as harbingers of this. The complementary danger is the tyranny of a minority, which is able to remake a society as the embodiment of its own values, even against the beliefs and preferences of a democratic majority, similarly claiming to be the arbiter of what is the good and true without having to accommodate those who think and know differently. Common to both tendencies is an assumption that these are matters to be resolved politically and legislatively *against* "the losers", as if, with a particular outcome secured, they will go away and leave the new settlement undisturbed.

Williams contrasts tribalism with tradition, as it is understood by the great religions. This is not "the conventional modern understanding" of tradition "as static and beyond argument", or the understanding of religious tribalism which reduces tradition to a series of "claims to timelessly valid, instantly accessible truths" demanding obedience and enforced by sanctions, but "a mode of prolonged learning and exposure to the truth". The approach to learning is the decisive factor in Williams's account of tribalism. It is easy to flatter ourselves about our openness to constant learning and ideas that are strange or disconcerting. In fact, it entails "an unwelcome strenuousness" and "an acceptance of ongoing difficulty", because it means that "the truth or rightness of a consensus" is never established or settled once and for all. Learning is "bound up with inherited and internalised habits of seeing and representing" which "have proved trustworthy and sustainable", and these habits of knowing "encounter difficulty and frustration" when confronted with different experiences and ways of seeing and representing which are outside their control. The encounter with the other and their different habits of knowing is a disturbance to what we thought was clear and complete because it cannot be readily contained within our own frame of reference. At this point, we can choose to accept that "exhaustive, final, definitive" knowledge is beyond us, that "there is always more to see and more to learn", allowing "new habits and strategies" of knowing to emerge "to modify what has been taken for granted" or previously thought to be adequate. Or, we can resist the work of "protracted learning", opting instead "to maximise the area of what is taken to be obviously and timelessly true," to treat the taken-for-granted as self-evident or given, and to repudiate the proposition that "engagement with the alien and unplanned is a potential source of insight and enrichment".

Tribalism, in short, is determined by a fundamental refusal to learn from the other. More than this, it holds that there is nothing that can be learnt from the other. Part of the paradox of political tribalism is that it regards what is outside itself as tribal. For the Enlightenment and for modernity, "the 'tribal' is that which is doomed because it has failed to change". It belongs to the past. It "is essentially over, and its persistence is an anomaly". The attitudes and behaviours it preserves are "aberrations from the norm", "destined for extinction", and "efforts to eradicate [them] can be seen as part of a struggle for fullness of human experience". Persistence in beliefs and ways of life which refuse to conform to enlightened or modern convictions, particularly if this persistence rises to doubt or denial of these convictions, is treated at best as "sub-rational" or as "a mark of mental or spiritual enslavement", and at worst as malign. How else to explain the refusal to embrace the obvious demands of wisdom, justice, and compassion reflected in an expanding number of moral and social positions in democratic societies? What is there to learn from other ways and habits of knowing which offer different perspectives—or worse, different conclusions—about these moral and social positions? Engagement with the other in these circumstances, if it does take place, can only be on the basis of suspicion or condescension.

The critical difference between tribalism and tradition centres on their relationship to truth. The truth for tribalism is a possession, complete and more or less final. For tradition, however, truth is not something we possess but an unfolding that we can enter into more and more deeply, the more willing we are to accept discipleship, "the status of a learner". Two very different approaches to what is legitimate and illegitimate in social and political life flow from this. For Enlightenment tribalism, the source of legitimacy lies in being modern, which in contemporary circumstances means revering technology and autonomy as the completion of human existence. Accompanying this is "the tacit belief that history has an automatic moral, value-laden direction, such that the pre-modern and the non-modern have no real legitimacy". Its genuine inability to comprehend how it is possible for some people not to embrace the timelessly self-evident truth of modernity, unless it is because of stupidity, manipulation, or malice, inevitably shrinks "the scope of mutual recognition" on which the formation of any sort of shared language or life in common depends. It narrows the possibilities for understanding "the 'investment' of the stranger" in their beliefs and ways of knowing, "the 'grammar' of [their] moral energy", and the basis it provides for intelligent action, which are among the key "factors that make us see problems differently". Closing off the interest and willingness to undertake "this labour of recognition" reduces public discourse to a contest of power, and fosters a political dynamic of "systematically and deliberately not recognising the claim of fellow human beings". Williams observes that the inexorable movement within political tribalism "towards delegitimising the other in debate" is "a fertile seedbed for totalitarianism", which embodies this refusal of recognition most drastically, and in doing so abandons "any intelligible claim to legitimacy" itself.

Just as exclusion underpins legitimacy for tribalism, recognition underpins legitimacy for tradition. For political tribalism, the factors which make the other see things differently are deformative. They prevent them from seeing the one and only truth, leaving them incompletely human. For tradition, incompletion is the nature of the human condition, not a diminishment or deprivation. The fully human is always incomplete and knowledge is always imperfect. To whatever extent it may be possible to inch towards anything like completeness or perfection, it is through patient, attentive engagement with the other and recognising in them an incompleteness like our own. From this, we may be able to discover something, even in the midst of fundamental disagreement. Tradition is directed towards the truth, not towards relativism or syncretism, but its "acceptance of an always incomplete and developing understanding" fosters "caution about supposing we have access to final certainty simply as individuals equipped with the tools of reasoning". This makes recognition of the other—even the opponent—and learning from them, easier. It places an emphasis on relationship and dependence, on giving time to listen to "the memory of discovery and conviction that lies behind an opponent's view", and to recognising in the arguments they make and the actions they take "comparable kinds of moral energy" to our own. It also establishes as a fundamental presupposition that "the other, even the opponent, has a continuing presence and stake in a shared social territory".

Perhaps it is the idea of shared territory that is most at risk from unbridled political tribalism, and with it the idea of a territory outside politics. Engagement with opponents will always entail critical exploration of each other's perspective. The crucial question is whether this is done for the purpose of delegitimising opponents and excluding them from a life in common, or with some genuine curiosity and willingness to learn, based not only on the recognition of shared humanity but on the assumption of a joint investment in a shared future. Following Aristotle, this latter course might be described as politics as a form of friendship.[1] Universal friendship is, of course, an impossibility, and, in Aristotle's account, a general friendliness or concord is the weakest form of friendship. Given how deeply riven our societies are becoming, how strange and hostile we sometimes appear to each other, embracing even the weakest form of friendship as a basis for our politics would be a significant step in a better direction. Instead of suspicion, delegitimisation, mutual incomprehension, and a creeping denial of the humanity—or at least the equality—of the other, politics as a form of friendship re-orients communal life towards liberality, generosity, and a shared concern for each other's flourishing. It makes it possible to conceive of a life in common in which technology and autonomy are subordinated to the service of an enriched and meaningful human existence, rather than substituting for it as ends in themselves. It does not extinguish disagreement, contestation, and conflict, but places them in a setting where they might be better constrained rather than barely checked, and where they might just yield something fruitful—such as learning and understanding—rather than the escalating enmity that political tribalism brings, with so much damage to communities and institutions.

To think of politics as friendship is itself a way of reminding ourselves that there is life outside it; that there are things beyond the political which are more important. Williams refers to Lord Acton's observation "that religious liberty was not just an *instance* of political liberty but its foundation", because "a state acknowledging freedom of religious belief and behaviour is acknowledging that it is not the sole measure of the identity of its citizens", who "may quite properly" consider themselves "as answerable to something more than the commands of a superior political power". From this flow all the critical hallmarks of a free society, including respect for conscience and minorities. In a similar way, "the most significant kinds of human solidarity do not derive from or depend on the state", and cannot be replaced by the state. Civic life depends on identities, convictions, and solidarities beyond civic life. For this reason, among others, Williams cautions against "the idea of the 'enlightened' state as universal arbiter of conviction". Instead,

> the presence in complex and pluralist societies of certain groups holding themselves accountable to more than an immediate social consensus is something democratic societies should be glad of: it keeps fundamental argument alive and obliges settled secular perspectives to articulate argument and justification for what they take for granted.

This itself is a work of friendship, undertaken not to justify a different position or to win an argument or to dispute the legitimacy of the views it challenges, but to help make a shared life sustainable.

Father James Schall SJ reminds us "that while there are things that transcend politics, it remains true that politics can, if not properly organized, serve to deflect or deform the human good. When this happens, it becomes of primary importance that bad regimes be changed".[2] Political tribalism is a symptom of deformation in otherwise good political and social regimes which seek to make it possible for people to flourish. Rather than treating this as a destiny, we should draw courage from the acute analysis Lord Williams has provided of this threat to our life in common, and choose change.

12

Refusing the Politics of Despair

Scott Stephens

Rowan Williams's account of our political malaise should be understood, I believe, as the further expression of a project that commenced in the mid-1990s, when he began developing a number of lines of thought that would be gathered together in that extraordinary essay, *Lost Icons: Reflections on Cultural Bereavement*.[1] The central concern of this project, as I read it, is to explore the conditions that are most conducive for the growth, stability, and survival of truly *human* community—a task which entails, necessarily, also identifying those patterns of behaviour and forms of life and habits of speech that diminish our souls and thence impair our capacity to live together. Looking back over the last twenty years, what Williams has managed to develop, gradually, tentatively, by means of a series of provocative, occasional interventions in public debates and through sustained conversations with figures as diverse as Augustine and Hegel, Shakespeare and Dostoevsky, Ludwig Wittgenstein and Simone Weil, Thomas Merton and Marilynne Robinson, Gillian Rose and Richard Sennett, is nothing less than a kind of *theology of culture*: a vision of our common life—its high and low moments, its occasions of heedless play and acute vulnerability, its poetry and its pedagogy, its language and its laws, its art and its commerce, its displays of erotic love and responses to ecological degradation—that fully *lives into* (to use Herbert McCabe's invaluable term of ethical discrimination)[2] the reality of human finitude, materiality, contingency, and interdependence.

In his latest intervention on the problem of political tribalism, the particular question that elicits my interest is what role Williams sees democratic politics playing in that vision of human community. Is it conducive, or is it corrosive? Does it (or can it) express a human aspiration for friendship, justice, and mutual discovery (and, if so, under what conditions), or is it so thoroughly enmired in partisan conflict and debased by the unprincipled pursuit of short-term electoral advantage that the best we can hope for now is to minimise its malign effects on our common life? Political division and persistent moral conflict have, of course, been preoccupying concerns for the former Archbishop of Canterbury and current crossbench member of the House of Lords—from the deep disagreements that continue to rack the Anglican communion, to the religious and ethnic tensions that intermittently flare and fade in multicultural societies like Britain, to the Brexit referendum and the ensuing chaos that consumed British politics for the better part of the last four years. But what is perhaps most striking about the way Williams has tried to address these divisions,[3] whether in the church, in politics, or in society, is how little concerned he is with their resolution. Far more important to him than resolving a moral disagreement, for example, is clarifying the conditions that would allow that disagreement to continue. The true danger, for Williams, is not that disagreement becomes interminable, but that it becomes incommensurable—which is to say, that both parties become locked in a state of mutual unintelligibility. This is why Williams's counsel is invariably for both sides to resolve to "stay alongside" one another, to take the time gradually to begin discerning the "elements of common language", or what he calls in this lecture "the 'grammar' of another's moral energy." This process of growing to recognise, as Williams frequently puts it, that "the other is not going away" and that their moral investment is in some way commensurate with one's own, establishes the conditions for what he calls "intelligent" or "intelligible action", which he describes elsewhere as:

> action capable of being talked about, action that is not the assertion of blind will, but is bound up with exchanges and negotiations that constitute a pattern of language. 'Intelligible action' is action that can be criticised and defended, understood or misunderstood. To borrow an idiom of Wittgenstein's, it is action that can be 'followed'.[4]

It is through this commitment to "unpressured listening", attentiveness, and mutual questioning that a path opens up: a transformation takes place which could not have been anticipated in advance, as both parties discover a kind of horizon of common experience or longing or action, and this recognition gives rise, in turn, to "forms of human solidarity and exchange" that "do not depend on identifying enemies" (which would be the likelihood were this a political resolution) and "are not so driven as to find no time for mutual listening" (as it would be if the disagreement was resolved by law). There is no objective process—like 'History' or 'Truth' or 'Progress'—at work here. What there is, rather, is *learning*, so that what was initially taken to be an impediment to one's plans or a challenge to what one believes to be self-evidently "given", comes to be seen instead as an invitation, a "potential source of insight and enrichment."[5] The crucial point for Williams, however, is that this kind of learning cannot be the work of politics or law, but only of a culture that is "confident, trustful enough to give time for perspectives to interact and interrogate one another and themselves."

Because Williams locates the moral labour involved in this process of learning and growth squarely within the purview of culture, it falls then to politics to cultivate an environment "that is capable of containing disagreement" and to manage change "in ways that do not violently disrupt the life of a society." This reflects a conception of the state—which he calls "pluralist", derived in no small measure from his reading of the nineteenth-century German philosopher G. W. F. Hegel, and refracted through the work of the early twentieth-century Anglican historian and political philosopher, J. N. Figgis, and English theologian David Nicholls[6]—whose role it is to "create the conditions, within a complex social environment, that allow each group to pursue what it sees as good."[7] But lest society be thought of as little more than the "juxtaposition of mutually non-communicating groups",[8] Williams understands the state as acting as a kind of arbiter, or, as he puts in this lecture, "a broker of interests between a natural diversity of local and voluntary networks of affiliation." This reflects his commitment to *interactive pluralism*: a way of ordering our common life which allows "active partnership and exchange between communities themselves and between communities and state authority."[9]

If this highly condensed summary begins to fill out what it might mean, for Williams, for politics to be conducive to a particular vision of human community, then some of the ways in which politics might severely repress culture's morally transformative or generative capacities likewise become clear. It is in his reading of Russian novelist Fyodor Dostoevsky, above all, that Williams discerns the threat that a certain form of political necessity—what we would call totalitarianism—will bring about "the corruption and eventual disappearance of politics itself":

> When dialogue fails, when history is supposed to be over, when certain aspects of the human mind have been recatalogued as pathologically generated illusions, there is no more politics: there is nothing to entertain dialogue *about*; nature, in the guise of a definitive account of what human beings timelessly need and how to meet those needs, has defeated culture.[10]

For Williams, Dostoevsky's animating concern is therefore the preservation of the conditions of humanity's survival, "not merely as a biological but as a cultural reality." And it is in this context, perhaps, that we find Williams's best account of what he understands truly *human* culture to be: it is a culture that "insists upon a recognition of mortality and fallibility, of limit, of mutual indebtedness for our nurture and psychological growth, of the inaccessibility of our souls to one another and of the gratuitousness and creative nature of what we say to one another."[11] If the task of politics, then, is to cultivate the conditions in which humans can exist as a cultural reality, any form of politics that "shrinks the scope of mutual recognition", or that "delegitimises the other in debate" as being somehow sub-rational and, therefore, beneath contempt, or that diminishes our capacity to "respond with either respect or compassion to each other" such that we have nothing significant left to say or learn, or that assumes that "the interesting questions have been answered and what remains is only an assortment of ways for whiling away the time"—all recognisable features of contemporary political discourse—represents, according to Williams, the denial of politics itself.[12] This is then what leads him to draw the inner connection between what he calls "intellectual modernity", political tribalism, totalitarianism, and majoritarian tyranny: each one just another variation on the same anti-human theme.

Williams's description of the nature of moral disagreement and its necessary non-resolution is compelling and, I think, wholly correct; as is the emphasis he places on the time-taking activities of "unpressured listening" and what we might call *purposive yet open-ended* attentiveness to the other in the process of learning. But notice that attention here is not a mere strategy for securing another's consent (by, say, making them 'feel' that they've been heard), or a more effective way of realising some predetermined project, political or otherwise (in which case any interest the other may hold for me vanishes once their role in my design is over). Truly attending to others, and opening oneself to the possibility of moral encounter, requires nothing less than relinquishing the very inclination to use them as a means to one's own end—which is to say, echoing the Jewish philosopher, Simone Weil, it demands a willingness to suspend all goals for the sake of understanding and in the hope of mutual transformation: "I do not attend to them *for* anything at all; my attention is an expression of my attempt to understand—to understand both them and myself, because . . . I cannot understand myself except through my understanding of others."[13] Hence why, as Weil insisted, attentiveness, like consent, like justice itself, is finally a work of love.[14]

What convinces me less is the way Williams wants culture to carry the entire moral charge, if you like, of the life of a political community, and grants politics some moral standing only to the extent that it sticks to its "arbitrative and balancing function."[15] I think this both undervalues the moral distinctiveness of democratic politics and ignores the chastening effect of democracy's peculiar pedagogy on our common life: the way, for example, it alters the nature of power by subordinating its exercise to popular sanction and constitutional control; or the way that democratic accountability necessarily tempers the ambitions of those who seek and those who wield power; or the way democracy's ennobled concept of 'individuality' elevates *conversation*, or the answerability of each to all, to what the American philosopher, Stanley Cavell, calls the "conditions of democratic morality" (Mark Twain's playful dethroning of 'majesty'—which is but another term, surely, for unanswerability—through the ruse of characters trading places with each another in books like *The Prince and the Pauper* and *Pudd'nhead Wilson*, is a powerful expression of this unmistakeably democratic sentiment).[16] That these are all moral achievements, or at least aspirations, made possible by a certain political vision, should not be minimised. Williams is right to stress the reciprocal and, indeed, even the redemptive relationship of culture to politics, such that, he hopes, the dedication of civic institutions and faith communities to nurturing forms of open-handed solidarity and rigorous communal self-scrutiny may yet help "salvage an intelligent, compassionate, and pluralist democracy from the wreckage of so much contemporary political habit." But by so dramatically narrowing the scope of what politics can contribute to the moral conditions of our common life—what might be called the cultivation of a truly democratic culture—I fear that Williams is, wittingly or not, giving succour to a certain fashionable contempt for politics as such. This is an imbalance that I think needs to be redressed if we are to stand any chance of escaping our political morass.

It begins with the recognition that politics, going back to Plato and Aristotle, is not primarily about power or action or responsibility, or even necessarily about order; it is, rather, a matter of culture, just to the extent that to do politics is *to cultivate the conditions of commonality*. Politics is what emerges, we could say, out of a people's concern to care for their common life: it is "a cultivating, a tending, a taking care of beings and things."[17] I find it at once significant and singularly instructive that political philosophers as different as Michael Oakeshott, a sceptical conservative, and Sheldon Wolin, a radical democrat, should both employ the pastoral image of "tending" or "attending" the shared life of a people "whom chance or choice have brought together" when describing the fundamental concern of politics,[18] not least because such a description gives us a welcome respite from the widespread sentiment that politics is inherently self-interested, unprincipled, brutal. This jaundiced view, while certainly not new, has acquired an almost unassailable hold on the popular imagination—and little wonder, when it is endlessly reiterated by the pornographic nihilism of shows like *House of Cards* and *Game of Thrones*, for example, and by the media's insatiable appetite for the *Lear*-like madness of the Trump administration. And when the same sentiment is then reinforced by many political journalists' undisguised admiration of the cunning of unelected party strategists (the figure early twentieth-century German sociologist Max Weber once called the "boss"—namely, an operative who is "completely without convictions and is interested only in how to attract votes")[19] or by their use of unjustifiably lurid language when reporting on otherwise nonviolent political contests, inner-party turmoil, and leadership spills ('war', 'war room', 'all-out war', 'knifing', 'night of the long knives', 'killing', 'killing off', 'killing season', 'blood on the floor', 'blood-letting', and so on, *ad nauseam*).

This cynical acceptance of the indecency of politics is meant to signal a kind of disabused realism about how politics really works and about the type of person who is drawn to public life. But, as I've already intimated, I think it is better seen as a form of contempt, insofar as it raises "every other realm of life above that of politics", as the legendary British journalist, Henry Fairlie, once wrote dismayingly of the self-congratulatory tone of political journalism in the aftermath of Watergate.[20] Like all forms of contempt, lurking behind this conceit that "no one is more base than the politician" is a perfidious moral vanity which takes a certain delight in the diminished standing of another because of the position of relative moral superiority one gains by comparison, at least in one's own eyes. But, again like all forms of contempt, such self-aggrandisement comes only ever at a profound cost, both to our souls and to our common life. For contemptuous eyes, if I can put it this way, are blind to reality, to what truly *is*; contempt causes the bloated self (what the philosopher, Iris Murdoch, unforgettably called the "fat relentless ego") to loom too large, even as it "withers" the object of its gaze.[21] It permits no "interval of hesitation" in the presence of the reality of another, precisely because it denies the other a reality, a depth of experience.[22] Which is to say, contempt is the opposite of attention. By sacrificing the complexity, the ethical particularity of the other on the altar of the ego, contempt encloses the self in a lie.[23] (I shall return to this point at the end.)

But unlike mere arrogance or pride, contempt is not just felt—it must be communicated. To put it bluntly: those contemned must be defamed. It is this tendency that gives contempt a kind of moral affect, the pretence of seriousness. So the eighteenth-century moral philosopher, Immanuel Kant, remarked with some horror on the "fiendish joy" that accompanies the dissemination or publicisation (he uses the Latin term *propalatio*) of the faults of others—particularly those we might call 'public' or 'representative' figures—and the way this casts "a shadow of worthlessness" over humanity as a whole and our common capacity to strive towards the good, thereby making "misanthropy . . . or contempt the prevalent cast of mind."[24] As Kant recognised, contempt precipitates a politics of despair. He therefore deemed it a "duty of virtue":

> not to take malicious pleasure in exposing the faults of others so that one will be thought as good as, or at least not worse than, others, but rather to throw the veil of philanthropy [*Menschenliebe*] over the faults, not merely by softening our judgments but also by keeping these judgments to ourselves; for examples of respect that we give others can arouse their striving to deserve it.[25]

Fairlie's criticism of the state of political journalism in the United States in the dying days of Gerald Ford's presidency is strikingly resonant with Kant on this point. For Fairlie, journalists as a profession bought into the conceit "that politics is probably if not necessarily ignoble" in order to promote their own cultural standing and better sell their wares.[26] This contempt for politics, self-serving as it was, could not help but erode an underlying democratic hopefulness—the joint conviction, as Fairlie put it, that "democracy is the accumulation of the moral aspirations and decisions of vexed but hopeful individuals", and that "politicians as such, however many individuals amongst them are venal or stupid, are the most hopeful messengers of a society's will to improve."[27] While such sentiments will no doubt be dismissed these days as inexcusably naïve, perhaps even irresponsible in a time when deep-seated distrust of elected officials and of the motivations and competence of voters (especially those on 'the other side' of the partisan divide) has been elevated to a kind of moral obligation, I think Fairlie was right to regard such hopefulness to be less an article of blind political faith than it is the condition of possibility for all other forms of political participation. Democratic hope, to put it simply, is the expression of our interdependence, the form of our commitment to the discovery of a shared horizon of interests and aspirations. What is contempt for politics, and indeed for politicians, but a bad-faith attempt to deny one's stake in the state of our common life in the name of a spurious moral superiority?

Of course, none of this is to dispute—who would do so?—that democratic politics is often more concerned with the accumulation of power than with its wise use; or that power-holders are drawn, irresistibly it seems, to unaccountability; or that politicians frequently veer into graft and calculated deception; or that political rhetoric, far from ennobling us or allaying our fear of and disdain for one another, increasingly appeals to the most petty and meanest of human sentiments, stoking them, coddling them, indulging and finally plunging them into an intensity they otherwise mightn't have reached; or that voters are too often guided more by fear, ignorance, and self-interest in their decision-making than they are by hope. These aspects of our current political culture are indeed egregious, and the damage they inflict on our common life mustn't be minimised or waved away. I don't think the famed American philosopher, John Dewey, was exaggerating when he said that anything which foments intolerance and mutual suspicion, anything which "bars freedom and fullness of communication" and "sets up barriers that divide human beings into sets and cliques, . . . antagonistic sects and factions", should be regarded as a form of "treason to the democratic way of life."[28] But that just underscores the extent to which we have something like an obligation, to one another, *not* to succumb to cynicism ('that's just politics'), but rather to dismiss these failures as so many abdications of the essential task of politics itself—namely, to 'tend' or 'cultivate' the conditions of commonality; to nurture those practices which are themselves inseparable from the democratic aspiration, like communal gathering, truthful speech, self-questioning, moral hesitation, compromise, and patience. For, as Dewey recognised, it is precisely the "day by day adoption" of such practices and their "contagious diffusion in every phase of our common life" which enables democracy to become a moral reality.[29]

Drawing these threads together: if we try to see politics and culture as being reciprocally constituted in this way—which is, I think, not vastly different from Rowan Williams's account, but different enough—we begin to get a fuller sense of what kind of politics it would be that could justly claim a certain moral legitimacy. It would be a way of organizing our common life and coordinating certain activities for common purpose, which nonetheless refuses to reduce citizens to mere means to some predetermined end. It would be a way of addressing shared problems that does not seek simply to solve them, but that sees the cultivation of mutual understanding and, ultimately, consent as inseparable from the solution itself. It would be a way of chastening the exercise of political authority—such that, for those who hold power, it is "at every moment, a temporary and conditional grant, regularly revocable"; and for those whose party or faction failed to secure an electoral majority, even defeat affords the opportunity to see the shared life and concerns of the political community through the lens of a different "moral emphasis or colouration."[30] It would be a politics that cultivates a preparedness to sacrifice, but that refuses to allow sacrifices to be born disproportionately by the most vulnerable. It would be a politics that nurtures an expansive notion of responsibility, a bounded sense of moral indeterminacy, and an openness to the possibility of "second chances."[31] It would, finally, be a politics that refuses the short-term expedience of a kind of boorish pragmatism which mistakes governance for dominating the news cycle and is content to skim opportunistically across the "surface of daily events", as the post-war German philosopher, Hannah Arendt, once put it (adding, "so that what is ballyhooed today always directly contradicts what happened yesterday"), but instead draws from the "wellsprings of human community" its moral coherence—the underlying "principle" of its action.[32]

There's a wonderful moment at the beginning of Frank Capra's *Mr Smith Goes to Washington* (1939). Governor Hubert 'Happy' Hopper (Guy Kibbee) is pacing back and forth in his study, agonising over whether to pick Horace Miller ("a born stooge") or Henry Hill (a "crackpot" idealist) to fill the vacancy left by a recently deceased senator. Unwilling to defy the wishes of either of the party factions lobbying for their man, and with his nerves "strained to the breaking point", in desperation he flips a coin: "Heads—Hill. Tails—Miller." The coin lands on its edge, resting against a small pile of newspapers. His eyes alight on a headline praising the deeds of the leader of Boy Rangers, a small-town hero named Jefferson Smith (Jimmy Stewart). "That's good enough for me", Hopper exclaims and races from the room. This moment when, as we might say, Fortuna intervenes by choosing *neither* of the candidates-at-hand, ought to cast doubt on the prevailing sense that the film is about what "one good man" can achieve in the otherwise debauched arena of democratic politics. It is just as easily about what "one good man" cannot achieve—after all, the only agency Smith brings with him to Washington is a kind of purity of desire and what Stanley Cavell describes as a "willingness for suffering", but little else besides.[33] What the failed coin-flip and Jefferson Smith's unlikely appointment to the Senate reveal, instead, is just the reality of the pre-existing political conditions. The waves of graft and sectional interest break against Smith; his presence merely makes them visible. Had the coin fallen on one side or the other, the *status quo ante* would have continued. Which is why, brass bands and ballyhoo boys notwithstanding, Capra's film is finally an expression of political despair—what little hope it does express in the capacity of democratic politics to pursue a good in common is as thin as the edge of a coin.

It is instructive to think about the twin epistemological shocks of 2016 which precipitated our own moment of widespread democratic despair—the election of Donald Trump and the result of the Brexit referendum—in similar terms. Both were effectively coin-flips, so narrow were the margins of victory; but both are said to represent the incursion of something alien, unwanted, unenlightened, old, into democracy's otherwise benign functioning: in the first instance, the stirrings of fascism; atavistic nationalism, in the second. This conceit has given rise to an entire industry devoted to exploring and exploiting the purported similarities between our time and the years leading up to the Second World War: from the steady stream of books (now almost comprising a sub-genre in its own right) identifying the tell-tale signs of fascism, to the renewed cultural interest in novels like George Orwell's

Nineteen Eighty-Four, Philip Roth's *The Plot Against America*, and Ray Bradbury's *Fahrenheit 451*.[34] I indicated earlier that I wanted to return to the suggestion that contempt encloses the self in a lie. And here, I think, we have a prime instance of the kind of self-deception which contempt engenders. The tendency to assign blame for our democratic decline to certain 'bad actors'—who are both accused of a kind of anti-democratic seizure of power, and then rendered as sub-human and therefore beneath contempt (I think here particularly of Ian McEwan's execrable novella, *The Cockroach*, and, to a lesser degree, Howard Jacobson's satire, *Pussy*)—who must be expunged in order for democratic politics to get back to 'normal', absolves of us any need to admit our own complicity in the communicative breakdown and habits of mutual inattentiveness which created the ideal conditions for the political paroxysms we call 'Trump' and 'Brexit'. Neither Donald Trump nor Boris Johnson is to blame for our malaise; they merely make the reality of our condition visible. As Yale intellectual historian Samuel Moyn recently put it, "Comparison to Nazism and fascism imminently threatening to topple democracy distracts us from how we made Trump over decades."[35]

The same year that *Mr Smith Goes to Washington* appeared on screen, and little more than a month after Germany invaded Poland, John Dewey wrote a brief address on the challenges that face democracy. Though alarmed by the rise of Hitler, he said that denouncing Nazism for its

> intolerance, cruelty and stimulation of hatred amounts to fostering insincerity if, in our personal relations to other persons, if, in our daily walk and conversation, we are moved . . . by anything save a generous belief in their possibilities as human beings, a belief which brings with it the need for providing conditions which will enable these capacities to reach fulfilment.[36]

What Dewey calls "democratic faith" is here a kind of

restatement of that conviction, going back to Plato and Aristotle, that politics—the task of tending or attending to the life of the *polis*—is the work of words. The city is, above all, a space for conversation (hence Dewey's claim, to which I've already alluded, that any act which divides the common life into "antagonistic sects and factions" is itself an act of treason). Unlike so many other pundits who rushed in to explain the threat Trump poses to democratic politics, Australian philosopher Raimond Gaita captures the moral dimensions of that threat with characteristic insight:

> Trump has destroyed the conversational space in which Americans can seriously disagree about their opinions and politics. The deepest reason why this is so, is not that he has divided them into camps fiercely opposed in their beliefs, though he has. Nor is it because he has inflamed passion to throw reason into a ditch, though he has. It is because he has eroded the conditions under which people can call their fellow citizens to seriousness . . .[37]

This is deeply consonant with Rowan Williams's emphasis on the importance of discovering a shared language in which we can both recognise and register one another's moral intensity. And it should serve to remind us that the word 'conditions' already implies the practices of *listening-to* and *speaking-with* one another—which is, after all, what the Latin verb *condicere* means. But it should also make us acutely aware that those politicians, paid-up partisan hacks and platform capitalists, who seem recently to have divined particular electoral or commercial advantage in the use of divisive and deceptive language, cannot really be said to be responsible for our political malaise. In a very real sense, they merely happened upon conducive soil in which to sow the seeds of distrust, discord, disdain, and brute intimidation. It is we who prepared the ground, and it is we who greedily devoured the meagre harvest. As I have said, to the extent that there is blame to be apportioned, we must each claim our share. Even here, however, there is ground for democratic hope, because if the cause of our malaise is never remote from us, then neither is the cure. As Stanley Cavell put it, rather gnomically, in his ingenious commentary on Thoreau's *Walden*, "To locate ourselves in this maze, the first step is to see that we ourselves are its architects and hence are in a position to recollect the design."[38]

CONTRIBUTORS

Michael Casey is the director the PM Glynn Institute, Australian Catholic University's public policy think-tank.

Anthony Ekpo is a chaplain at Australian Catholic University's Rome campus and an official of the Vatican Secretariat of State.

Ben Etherington is a senior lecturer in postcolonial and world literary studies and a member of the Writing and Society Research Centre at Western Sydney University.

Cristina Lledo Gomez is the pastoral associate for staff at Australian Catholic University's North Sydney campus, Presentation Sisters Lecturer in Theology at BBI-The Australian Institute for Theological Education, and research fellow at Charles Sturt University's Public and Contextual Theology Research Centre.

Sandra Jones is a professor of health and social research and Pro Vice-Chancellor (Engagement) at Australian Catholic University. She is also an autistic woman and mother of two adult autistic children.

Annette Pierdziwol is a senior lecturer in philosophy and assistant director of the Institute for Ethics & Society, University of Notre Dame Australia.

Kerry Pinkstone is a visiting fellow at the PM Glynn Institute, having previously served as senior adviser on social policy in the Office of the Prime Minister during the premiership of the Honourable Malcom Turnbull MP.

Scott Stephens is the ABC's religion and ethics editor and co-host of The Minefield on ABC Radio National.

Amanda Stoker is a Senator for Queensland in the Parliament of the Commonwealth of Australia.

Ethan Westwood is an intern at the PM Glynn Institute and an undergraduate at the University of Wollongong.

Austin Wyatt is a research associate in the University of New South Wales's Values in Defence & Security Technology group at the Australian Defence Force Academy.

Nigel Zimmermann is principal advisor to the Catholic Archbishop of Melbourne, adjunct lecturer in the Institute for Ethics & Society, University of Notre Dame Australia, and a fellow of the PM Glynn Institute.

NOTES

Overcoming political tribalism

1 See, for example, the statement of Robert Ramsay in 1848, concerning his Aboriginal neighours: "The inferior must give way to the superior race, and, if this be so, . . . the subjugation—and, I very much fear, the extermination—of the black fellow must follow" (quoted in D. Freeman and S. Morris (eds),*The Forgotten People: Liberal and Conservative Approaches to Recognising Indigenous Peoples* (Melbourne University Press, 2016), p. 53).

2 For the background and recent discussion, see the Final Report of the Truth and Reconciliation Commission of Canada, volume 1: *Summary. Honouring the Truth, Reconciling for the Future* (James Lorimer and Co, 2015). On the Canadian residential schools, I must acknowledge my debt to the researches of the Reverend David Bryant-Scott.

3 On this theme of the temporal displacement of the 'other', see especially J. Fabian, *Time and the Other: How Anthropology Makes Its Object,* 2nd edn (Columbia University Press, 2014).

4 Recent instances would include the British referendum on exiting the European Union (which delivered a roughly four percentage-point majority) and the United States election of 2016 (where an absolute numerical majority nationwide in fact voted for the unsuccessful candidate). In both cases, subsequent political rhetoric has presented these as overwhelming popular endorsements, and there has been little or no attempt to frame policy in the light of the slenderness of the majority and the continuing needs and arguments of the 'losers', and it has to be said also that the unsuccessful minority has bought into the same absolutism and oppositional ferocity.

5 E.g. in "Arguments don't stop after a vote", *New Statesman,* 31 March-6 April 2017, pp. 40-41.

6 See G. Palast, *The Best Democracy Money Can Buy* (Pluto Press, 2002).

7 P. Whittaker, "The computer will see you now", *New Statesman,* 2-15 August 2019, pp. 39-43.

8 L. Wittgenstein, *Lectures and Conversations on Aesthetics, Psychology and Religious Belief,* ed. C. Barrett (Blackwell, 1966), pp. 24, 43-4, 51-2.

9 "Conclusion: Understanding where they're coming from" in Freeman and Morris, pp. 172-178.

10 Simon Baron-Cohen's *Zero Degrees of Empathy: A New Understanding of Cruelty and Kindness* (Penguin Books, 2012) provides some rather startling illustrations of the simplistic idea that 'empathy' alone is the solvent of all major moral and political conflicts.

11 I have in mind especially the work of John Milbank and Oliver O'Donovan.

12 Think here of the concerns raised by the insistence that there should be access to women-only facilities, or indeed women-only sports, by any individual self-identifying as female. It should be possible to understand the legitimate anxieties here and the need for negotiated problem-solving without compromising justice for transitioning or transitioned persons.

13 R. Bringhurst and J. Zwicky, *Learning to Die: Wisdom in the Age of Climate Crisis* (University of Regina Press, 2019), p. 87.

14 He is commenting on Pinker's *Enlightenment Now: The Case for Reason, Science, Humanism and Progress* (Penguin Books, 2018).

15 Bringhurst and Zwicky, p. 75.

16 See, e.g., Acton, *The History of Freedom and Other Essays,* ed. J.N. Figgis and R.V. Laurence (Macmillan, 1907), pp. 30ff.

17 Reflection on the conditions for 'just' resistance to unjust government (even by force) goes back to Aquinas's discussions of the subject see, e.g., *Summa theologiae* II. ii. 42, ad 3. In the twentieth century, Dietrich Bonhoeffer's wrestlings with this in his fragmentary *Ethics,* transl. by R. Krauss, C.C. West, and D.W. Stott (Fortress Press, 2005), Vol. 6 in the new complete translation of Bonhoeffer's works, have become a *locus classicus*; see especially pp. 246-298.

18 Especially those in the succession of Lord Acton, such as the Anglican political philosopher and theologian John Neville Figgis; the stress in twentieth-century Catholic social teaching on 'subsidiarity' is a closely related theme.

19 Hans-Georg Gadamer might be said to have begun this kind of revaluation of 'tradition' among social philosophers, echoed by Paul Ricoeur and Alasdair MacIntyre.

20 Bringhurst and Zwicky, pp. 49-66.

21 *Ibid.*, p. 66.

22 S. Weil, *Gravity and Grace* (Routledge and Kegan Paul, 1952), p. 105.

23 I take the phrase from F. Michel, *Etienne Gilson: Une biographie intellectuelle et politique* (Vrin, 2018), p. 319, where he characterises the work of the great philosophical historian and mediaevalist work as preserving "le sens de la longue duree chretienne, l'humilite de l'homme, et une feconde liberte."

The reasonable poet and the clamour of the crowd

1 As Williams says in his lecture, religious 'tradition' can only have credibility if it also has an investment in self-critical learning.

2 "Higher than the Cherubim . . .", as the fourth-century hymn to Mary the Theotokos (the 'God-bearer' or 'Mother of God', which today is repeated in the Divine Liturgy of Saint John Chrysostom, with its subtle reference to Psalm 8).

3 R. Williams, "Sermon at the International Mass in the Basilica of S. Pius X" in *Mary: A Focus for Unity for All Christians* (Taverner House, 2008), pp. 35-9.

4 R. Williams, *Lost Icons: Reflections on Cultural Bereavement* (Continuum, 2003).

5 Ibid., p. 160.

6 S. Weil. "Letter VI to her father" in *Waiting for God,* transl. E. Craufurd (Harper Perennial), p. 50.

Overcoming intellectual fragility

1 K. Bense, "How Politics in Trump's America Divides Families", *The Atlantic,* 26 November 2018.

2 M. Wright and E. Zolfagharifard, "Internet is giving us shorter attention spans and worse memories, major study suggests", *The Telegraph,* 6 June 2019.

3 Much has been said about the poor mental health of those who serve in politics. If the work of people like Brené Brown on the need for a person to be vulnerable as a precondition to forming genuine relationships and maintaining good mental health is anything to go by, our approach here is likely to be doing harm to the individual participants in politics as well as to the bigger picture of tribalism.

4 G. Lukianoff and J. Haidt, "The Coddling of the American Mind", *The Atlantic,* September 2015.

5 M.L. King Jr, "I have a dream" (1963), see <https://www.archives.gov/files/press/exhibits/dream-speech.pdf>.

6 "John Howard's acceptance speech", *Sydney Morning Herald*, 10 October 2004.

Tribalism as anti-politics

1 E. Humphrys, "We Live in Anti-political Times", *Overland,* 20 May 2019.

Are shared languages enough?

1 *Aristotle, The Politics of Aristotle*, transl. B. Jowett, (Clarendon Press, 1885), 2 vols.

2 See Pope Francis, Video Message for the Meeting of Catholic Politicians Serving the Latin American Peoples, 1 December 2017.

3 The Second Vatican Council, Pastoral Constitution on the Church in the Modern World, Gaudium et Spes, no.74.

4 See Pope Francis's video message.

5 S. Kitayama and C.E. Salvador, "Culture Embrained: Going Beyond the Nature-Nurture Dichotomy", *Perspectives on Psychological Science*, 2017, Vol. 12(5), pp. 841-854.

6 A. Finlayson, "Stop Worrying About 'Tribalism': Politics is Supposed to be Passionate", *The Guardian,* 12 December 2019.

7 *Ibid.*

8 A. Chua and J. Rubenfeld, "The Threat of Tribalism", *The Atlantic*, October 2018.

9 *Ibid.*

10 J. Mumford, *Vexed: Ethics beyond Political Tribes* (Bloomsbury Continuum, 2020), p. 7.

11 *Ibid.*, p. 13.

12 S. Carter, *Civility: Manners, Morals and Etiquette of Democracy* (Harper Perennial, 1999).

13 *Ibid.*

14 Pope Paul VI, Address to the Commission for the Revision of the Code, 20 December 1965.

15 On the application of this phrase or principle to the law of the Catholic Church, see L. Örsy, "The Meaning of Novus Habitus Mentis: The Search for New Horizons", *The Jurist*, 1988, Vol. 48, pp. 429-447.

16 Örsy, p. 431.

17 *Ibid.*, p. 435.

18 L. Wittgenstein, *Philosophical Investigations* (Macmillan, 1985), §§54, 68 and 100.

19 D.M. High, *Language, Persons, and Belief: Studies in Wittgenstein's Philosophical Investigations and Religious Uses of Language* (Oxford University Press, 1967), p. 10.

20 See M. Coleridge, "Seeing the Faces, Hearing the Voices" in A. Ekpo and D. Pascoe (eds), *Words from the Wound: Selected Addresses, Letters and Homilies of Archbishop Mark Coleridge* (St Paul's Publications, 2014), pp. 203—212; see also D. Freeman and S. Morris, *The Forgotten People: Liberal and Conservative Approaches to Recognising Indigenous Peoples* (Melbourne University Press, 2016).

Overcoming tribalist colonialism

1 A.M. Brazal, "Postcolonialism" in W.T. Cavanaugh (ed), *The Wiley Blackwell Companion to Political Theology*, 2nd edn (Wiley Blackwell, 2019), pp. 516-530.

2 Other forms of oppression include exploitation, marginalisation, powerlessness, and cultural imperialism: see I.M. Young, "The Five Faces of Oppression" in *Justice and the Politics of Difference* (Princeton University Press, 2011), pp. 39-65. Oppression can be based on distinctive labels such as gender, race, or both, for example. The groups of people who usually fall into these categories include migrants, Aboriginal or First Peoples of nations, and the LGBT+ community.

3 David and Okazaki in S.O. Utsey, J.A. Abrams, A. Opare-Henaku, M.A. Bolden, O. Williams III, "Assessing the Psychological Consequences of Internalized Colonialism on the Psychological Well-Being of Young Adults in Ghana", *Jour-*

nal of Black Psychology, 2015, Vol. 41, pp. 195-220, p. 198.

4 *Ibid.*

5 K. Aquino, *Racism and Resistance Among the Filipino Diaspora: Everyday Anti-Racism in Australia* (Routledge, 2018), p. 59.

6 *Ibid.*

7 V.E. Tuazon, E. Gonzalez, D. Gutirrez, and L. Nelson, "Colonial Mentality and Mental Health Help-Seeking of Filipino Americans", *Journal of Counselling and Development*, 2019, Vol. 97, pp. 352-363.

8 *Ibid.*

9 See B. Rawson-Bridge, "Ceasefire Pauses Three-Year PNG Tribal War", RNZ (Radio New Zealand) website: <https://www.rnz.co.nz/international/pacific-news/412434/ceasefire-pauses-three-year-png-tribal-war>.

10 Paul VI, *On the Development of Peoples: Populorum Progressio, Papal Encyclical Letter* (1967).

11 Francis, *Instituting the Dicastery for promoting Integral Human Development, Apostolic Letter* (2016).

12 Benedict XVI, *On Integral Human Development in Charity and Truth: Caritas in Veritate, Papal Encyclical Letter* (2009), n. 11.

13 Francis, *Beloved Amazon: Querida Amazonia—Post-Synodal Apostolic Exhortation* (2020), paragraph 8.

14 See Synod of Bishops Special Assembly for the Pan-Amazonian Region, *The Amazon: New Paths for the Church and for an Integral Ecology—Final Document* (2019).

15 *Ibid.*, n. 9.

16 Francis, *Laudato Si: On Care for Our Common Home—Papal Encyclical Letter* (2015); *Querida Amazonia*, paragraph 36.

17 *Querida Amazonia,* n. 58.

18 *Ibid.*, paragraph 38.

19 *Ibid.*, paragraph 60.

20 *Ibid.*, paragraph 81.

21 *The Amazon Final Document,* n. 87.

22 The wolf will dwell with the lamb: Isaiah 11:6; under Jesus who is both the lion and the lamb, the conqueror and conquered/victim: Revelations 5:5-6.

Mutual recognition

1 C. Helmers, "Looking back on the Adam Goodes drama", Media Acadamy, Fox Sports.

2 G. Yunupingu, "Tradition, truth and tomorrow", *The Monthly,* December 2008.

3 "Perkins hoping to re-open Indigenous recognition dialogue in 2019 Boyer Lec-

tures", *Sydney Morning Herald,* 11 October 2019.

4 L. Pearson, "What is a Makarrata? The Yolngu word is more than a synonym for treaty", ABC News online, 10 August 2017.

5 C. Dow and J. Gardiner-Garden, *Overview of Indigenous Affairs: Part 1: 1901 to 1991* (Parliamentary Library, Australian Parliament House).

Orientalism, learning and tribalist violence

1 S. Keen, *Faces of the enemy: Reflections of the hostile imaginations* (Harper & Row, 1986).

2 A. Mohammadpour and K. Soleimani, "Interrogating the tribal: the aporia of 'tribalism'in the sociological study of the Middle East", *British Journal of Sociology,* 2019, Vol. 70(5), pp. 1799-1824.

3 M. Komel, "Re-orientalizing the Assassins in Western historical-fiction literature: Orientalism and self-Orientalism in Bartol's Alamut, Tarr's Alamut, Boschert's Assassins of Alamut and Oden's Lion of Cairo", *European Journal of Cultural Studies*, 2014, Vol. 17(5), pp. 525–548.

4 Ibid., p. 527.

5 E. Said, *Orientalism,* (Pantheon Books, 1972), p. 36.

6 E. Said, "Orientalism reconsidered", *Cultural critique*, 1985, Vol. 1, p. 102.

7 M. Haldrup, L. Koefoed and K. Simonsen, "Practical orientalism–bodies, everyday life and the construction of otherness", *Geografiska Annaler: Series B, Human Geography*, 2006, Vol. 88(2), pp. 173-184, p. 174.

8 F. Mégret, "From 'savages' to 'unlawful combatants': a postcolonial look at international law's 'other'" in A. Orford (ed.), *International Law and its 'Others'* (Cambridge University Press, 2006), p. 15.

9 *Ibid.*, p. 35.

10 "Orientalism reconsidered", p. 105.

11 R. Howson and K. Smith, "Hegemony and the Operation of Consensus and Coercion" in R. Howson and K. Smith (eds), *Hegemony: Studies in Consensus and Coercion*, (Routledge, 2008).

12 Mégret, p. 5.

13 Komel, p. 527.

14 E. Steuter and D. Wills, *At war with metaphor: media, propaganda, and racism in the war on terror* (Lexington Books, 2009), p. 45.

15 Komel, p. 535.

16 M. Foucault, *The History of Sexuality,* (Random House, 1978), p. 137.

17 M. Foucault, *Security, Territory, Population* (St Martin's Press, 2007), p. 1.

18 J. Duran, "Virtual borders, data aliens, and bare bodies: Culture, securitization, and the biometric state", *Journal of Borderlands Studies,* 2010, Vol. 25(3-4), p.

227.

19 F. Debrix and A. Barder, *Beyond biopolitics: theory, violence, and horror in world politics* (Routledge, 2013), p. 12.

20 G. Agamben, *"Homo Sacer: Sovereign Power and Bare Life"*, transl. by D. Heller-Roazen (Stanford University Press, 1998), p.74.

21 K. Grayson, "Biopolitics, culture and political violence", *Security Dialogue, 2012*, Vol. 43(1), p. 28.

22 M. Foucault, *Society Must be Defended* (St Martin's Press, 2003), p. xvii.

23 *Ibid.*, p. 257.

24 *Ibid.*, p. 258.

25 C. Federman, "A 'Morphological Sphinx': On the Silence of the Assassin Leon Czolgosz", *Journal of Theoretical and Philosophical Criminology*, 2010, Vol. 2(2), p. 102.

26 J. Jouhki, and H.-R. Pennanen, "The Imagined West: Exploring Occidentalism", Suomen antropologi, 2016, Vol. 41(2), pp. 1-10.

27 E. Wishnick, "In search of the 'Other' in Asia: Russia–China relations revisited", *The Pacific Review*, 2017, Vol. 30(1), pp. 114-132.

28 A.A. Moghadam, "We Other Spartans: Orientalism, Occidentalism and the Enemy Other Ancient Greece and Contemporary Wars", I*nternational Studies Journal*, 2017, Vol. 13(4), pp. 39-62.

29 F. Fukuyama, "Against Identity Politics: The New Tribalism and the Crisis of Democracy", *Foreign Affairs*, 2018, Vol. 97(5), pp. 90-115.

30 G. Bettiza and D. Lewis, "Authoritarian Powers and Norm Contestation in the Liberal International Order: Theorizing the Power Politics of Ideas and Identity", *Journal of Global Security Studies,* 2019.

31 S.E. Hobfoll, "Historical Threat and the Priming of Tribal Violence" in S.E. Hobfall (ed.), *Tribalism* (Palgrave Macmillan, 2018), pp. 77-100.

32 Z. Lockman, *Contending Visions of the Middle East: The History and Politics of Orientalism, 2nd edn* (New York University Press, 2010).

33 P. Vasunia, "Hellenism and Empire: reading Edward Said", *Parallax,* 2003, Vol. 9(4), pp. 88-97.

34 D. Nicolle, *Teutonic Knight: 1190-1561* (Osprey, 2007).

35 P. Rich, "European identity and the myth of Islam: a reassessment", *Review of International Studies*, 1999, Vol. 25, pp. 435-451.

36 Komel, p. 527.

37 M. Haldrup, L. Koefoed and K. Simonsen, above.

38 P. Rich, "European identity and the myth of Islam: a reassessment", *Review of* International Studies, 1999, Vol. 25, pp. 435-451.

39 D. Ahrens, "Christianity's Contribution to Just War Tradition", *Strategy Research Paper,* 30 March 1999 (United States Army War College Press), p. 10.

40 M. Howard, G. Andreopoulos and M. Shulman, *The Laws of War: Constraints on Warfare in the Western World* (Yale University Press, 1997), p. 29.

41 L. White Jr, "Technology assessment from the stance of a medieval historian", *Technological Forecasting and Social Change,* 1974, Vol. 6(1), p. 5.

42 Howard et al., p. 30.

43 Ahrens, p. 11.

44 R. Belfield, *Secret History of Assassination: The Killers and Their Paymasters Revealed* (Magpie Books, 2008).

45 Komel, p. 527.

46 D.A. Bell, *The First Total War: Napoleon's Europe and the birth of warfare as we know it* (Houghton Mifflin Harcourt, 2007).

47 P. Rich, "European identity and the myth of Islam: a reassessment", *Review of International Studies,* 1999, Vol. 25, pp. 435-451.

48 P. Dwyer, "'It Still Makes Me Shudder': Memories of Massacres and Atrocities during the Revolutionary and Napoleonic Wars", *War in History*, 2009, Vol. 16(4), pp. 381-405.

49 F. Mégret, *From 'savages' to 'unlawful combatants': a postcolonial look at international law's 'other'* (Œuvres completes, 1991), pp. 704-705.

50 C.J. Chivers, *The Gun: The AK-47 and the Evolution of War* (Penguin Books, 2013).

51 S. Lindqvist, *A history of bombing* (New Press, 2001), p. 48.

52 D. Gregory, "'In another time-zone, the bombs fall unsafely....': Targets, Civilians, and Late Modern War", *Arab World Geographer,* 2006, Vol. 9(2), p. 13.

53 Lindqvist, p. 57.

54 P. Satia, "The Defense of Inhumanity: Air Control and the British Idea of Arabia", *American Historical Review,* 2006, Vol. 111(1), pp. 29-40.

55 Z. Lockman, *Contending Visions of the Middle East: The History and Politics of Orientalism,* 2nd edn (New York University Press, 2010).

Digital tribalism

No notes

Defending the 'I' in tribe

1 On vaccinations, see L.E. Taylor, A.L. Swerdfeger, and G.D. Eslick, "Vaccines are not associated with autism: An evidence-based meta-analysis of case-control and cohort studies", *Vaccine,* 2014. Vol. 32(29), pp. 3623-3629; on refrigerator mothers, see S. Cohmer, "Early Infantile Autism and the Refrigerator Mother Theory (1943-1970)" in *Embryo Project Encyclopedia* (Arizona State University, 2014); on harmful 'treatments', such as chelation, see S. James et al., "Chelation for autism spectrum disorder (ASD)", Cochrane Database of Systematic Reviews, 2015; and on drinking chlorine dioxide (bleach), see B.

Houck, "FDA Warns Against Drinking Products That Falsely Claim to 'Cure Autism' and Actually Contain Bleach", *New York Times,* 13 August, 2019.

2 L. Kanner, "Autistic disturbances of affective contact", Nerv Child, 1943, Vol. 2(3), pp. 217-250; H. Asperger, "Die sutistischen Psychopathen im Kindesalter", *Archiv für Psychiatrie,* 1944, Vol. 117, pp. 76-136.

3 N. Hadjikhani, "Scientifically deconstructing some of the myths regarding autism", *Schweizer Archiv fur Neurologie und Psychiatrie,* 2014, Vol. 165, pp. 272-276.

4 S.K. Kapp et al., "Deficit, difference, or both? Autism and neurodiversity", *Developmental Psychology,* 2013, Vol. 49(1), pp. 59–71.

5 S. Knobloch-Westerwick, C. Mothes, and N. Polavin, "Confirmation Bias, Ingroup Bias, and Negativity Bias in Selective Exposure to Political Information", *Communication Research,* 2020, Vol. 47(1), pp. 104–124.

6 M. Jeong et al., "Feeling displeasure from online social media postings: A study using cognitive dissonance theory", *Computers in Human Behavior,* 2019, Vol. 97, pp. 231-240.

7 E. Pariser, "Beware online 'filter bubbles'", 2011, *TED: Ideas worth spreading.*

8 *How Filter Bubbles Distort Reality: Everything You Need to Know* (Farnam Street, 2017): online reading platform.

9 G. Vivanti, "Ask the Editor: What is the Most Appropriate Way to Talk About Individuals with a Diagnosis of Autism?", *Journal of Autism and Developmental Disorders,* 2019, Vol. 50, pp. 691-693.

10 L. Jones, "Don't fix me, I'm not broken", The Creativity Project (Big Fat Smile, 2013): <http://www.think-in-colour.com.au/2013/03/08/the-creativity-project/>.

11 L. Camm-Crosbie, et al., "'People like me don't get support': Autistic adults' experiences of support and treatment for mental health difficulties, self-injury and suicidality", *Autism,* 2018, Vol. 23(6), pp. 1431-1441.

12 J. Sinclair, *Don't mourn for us* (Autism Network, 1993).

13 M.A. Gernsbacher and M. Yergeau, "Empirical failures of the claim that autistic people lack a theory of mind", *Archives of Scientific Psychology,* 2019, Vol. 77(1), pp. 102-118.

14 O. Smith and S.C. Jones, "'Coming out' with Autism: Identity in People with an Asperger's Diagnosis after DSM-5", *Journal of Autism and Developmental Disorders,* 2020, Vol. 50, pp. 592-602.

Sustaining society

1 Williams's preference for the particular over the abstract has a long history in Western political philosophy, perhaps most paradigmatically seen in Edmund Burke's Reflections on the Revolution in France.

2 M.C. Nussbaum, *Political Emotions* (Harvard University Press, 2015), p. 16.

3 *Ibid.*, p. 9.

4 *Ibid.*, p.10.

5 *Ibid.*, p. 222.

6 *Ibid.*, p. 16.

7 *Ibid.*, pp. 4-5.

8 Nussbaum argues that Rawls himself had seen this need. She writes, "he insists he is leaving a space for a needed account of a "reasonable moral psychology." Nussbaum's Political Emotions aims to fill that space (p. 9).

9 *Political Emotions*, p. 15.

10 *Ibid.*, p. 11.

11 *Ibid.*, p. 223.

12 D.C. Batson, *Altruism in Humans* (Oxford University Press, 2011).

13 *Political Emotions,* p. 11.

14 *Ibid.*, p. 10.

15 See also, M.C. Nussbaum, *Not for Profit: Why Democracy Needs the Humanities, updated edn* (Princeton University Press, 2017).

16 *Political Emotions,* p. 295.

17 D. Hume, *A Treatise of Human Nature*, edited by D.F. Norton and M.J. Norton (Clarendon Press, 2000), §2.2.4.3; D. Hume, *A Treatise of Human Nature, 2nd edn,* edited by L.A. Selby-Bigge, revised by P.H. Nidditch, 2nd edn (Oxford University Press, 1978), p. 352.

18 Norton edn, §2.1.11.6; Selby-Bigge edn, p. 318.

19 Norton edn, §2.2.4.2; Selby-Bigge edn, p. 352.

20 For an overview of this evidence, see my "Cultivating Empathic Concern and Altruistic Motivation: Insights from Hume and Batson" in R. Vitz and P. Reed (eds), *Hume's Moral Philosophy* and *Contemporary Psychology* (Routledge, 2018), pp.142-169, especially pp.157-9.

21 See C.D. Batson, D.A. Lishner, J. Cook and S. Sawyer, "Similarity and Nurturance: Two Possible Sources of Empathy for Strangers, Basic and Applied", *Social Psychology*, 2005, Vol. 27, pp. 15–25. Batson et al. note that perceived similarity is "one of the explanations most frequently offered by personality and social psychologists for why we feel empathy for strangers" (p. 15). However, they argue that in their experiments they found "no evidence that perceived similarity accounts for the variability in empathy felt for strangers", suggesting instead that it may play a more modest role as a moderator rather than a source of empathic concern (p. 23).

22 A. Gopnik, "When Truth and Reason Are No Longer Enough: review of Steven Pinker, Enlightenment Now", *The Atlantic,* April 2018.

23 *Ibid.*

24 I would like to thank Tim Smartt for feedback on an earlier version of this essay.

Two concepts of legitimacy

1 Aristotle, Nicomachean Ethics, Book 8. The account here is drawn from J.V. Schall SJ, *The Order of Things* (Ignatius Press, 2007), pp. 125-27.

2 Schall, p. 127.

Refusing the Politics of Despair

1 R. Williams, *Lost Icons: Reflections on Cultural Bereavement* (Continuum, 2000).

2 H. McCabe, *What is Ethics All About?* (Corpus Books, 1969), p. 100.

3 See, for example, Williams's address to the plenary session of the 1998 Lambeth Conference, published as "On Making Moral Decisions", *Anglican Theological Review,* 1999, Vol. 81(2), pp. 295-308; and his 2008 lecture given to the Royal Courts of Justice, "Civil and Religious Law in England: A Religious Perspective", and published in R. Ahdar and N. Aroney (ed.), *Shari'a in the West* (Oxford University Press, 2010), pp. 293-303 (for an insightful treatment of the divisions Williams's lecture provoked, see T. Modood, "Multicultural Citizenship and the Shari'a Controversy in Britain", pp. 33-42 in the same volume). Most of Williams's interventions on the Brexit debate have appeared in the New Statesman, such as: "Brexit shows Britain is no longer able to imagine a 'common good'", *New Statesman,* 20 March 2019.

4 Rowan Williams, "Between Politics and Metaphysics: Reflections in the Wake of Gillian Rose" in M. Higton (ed.), *Wrestling with Angels: Conversations in Modern Theology* (Eerdmans, 2007), p. 57.

5 I suspect that what lay in the background here, along with Simone Weil's understanding of the other as "limit", is Thomas Merton's account of "the realism of nonviolence" which should make it impossible for a Christian to "generalise about 'the wicked' against whom he takes up moral arms in a struggle for righteousness. He will not let himself be persuaded that the adversary is totally wicked and can therefore never be reasonable or well-intentioned, and hence need be listened to." That's why, for Merton, the test of Christians' "sincerity in the practice of nonviolence is this: are we willing to learn something from the adversary?" See T. Merton, "Blessed Are the Meek: The Christian Roots of Nonviolence" in W.H. Shannon (ed.), *Passion for Peace: Reflections on War and Nonviolence* (Crossroad, 1995), pp. 95, 100.

6 See D. Nicholls, *The Pluralist State: The Political Ideas of J.N. Figgis and his Contemporaries,* 2nd edn (St Martin's Press, 1994).

7 R. Williams, "Law, Power and Peace" in his *Faith in the Public Square* (Bloomsbury, 2012), p. 50.

8 "Law, Power and Peace", p. 58.

9 *Ibid.,* p. 60; see also "Civil and Religious Law in England", p. 302.

10 R. Williams, *Dostoevsky: Language, Faith, and Fiction* (Baylor University

Press, 2008), pp. 236-7.

11 *Ibid.*, pp. 237-8.

12 See Williams, "Overcoming Political Tribalism"; Dostoevsky, p. 238; and "Europe, Faith and Culture" in *Faith in the Public Square*, p. 72.

13 P. Winch, *Simone Weil: "The Just Balance"* (Cambridge University Press, 1989), pp. 187-8.

14 S. Weil, "Are We Struggling for Justice?" in *Philosophical Investigations,* transl. M. Barabas, 10.1 (1987), pp. 6-7.

15 "Law, Power and Peace", p. 61.

16 The work of George Kateb is centrally important to this point; see in particular: "The Moral Distinctiveness of Representative Democracy" and "Democratic Individuality and the Claims of Politics", both in *The Inner Ocean: Individualism and Democratic Culture* (Cornell University Press, 1992), pp. 36-56, 77-105; "Individuality and Egotism" in B. Honig and D.R. Mapel (eds), *Skepticism, Individuality, and Freedom: The Reluctant Liberalism of Richard Flathman* (University of Minnesota Press, 2002), pp. 86-100; and "Democracy and Untruth", *Raritan*, 2012, Vol. 31(3), pp. 60-88. On the "conditions of democratic morality", see S. Cavell, *Conditions Handsome and Unhandsome: The Constitution of Emersonian Perfectionism* (University of Chicago Press, 1990), p. 125

17 S. Wolin, "Hannah Arendt: Democracy and the Political" in N. Xenos (ed.), *Fugitive Democracy and Other Essays* (Princeton University Press, 2016), p. 248.

18 M. Oakeshott, "Political Education" in *Rationalism in Politics and Other Essays* (Liberty Fund, 1991), p. 44.

19 M. Weber, "Politics as a Vocation" in D. Owen and T.B. Strong (eds), *The Vocation Lectures,* transl. Rodney Livingstone (Hackett, 2004), p. 70. A better way of characterizing what I've here blandly called "admiration" is Jay Rosen's description of "the cult of savviness": "In politics, our journalists believe, it is better to be savvy than it is to be honest or correct on the facts. It's better to be savvy than it is to be just, good, fair, decent, strictly lawful, civilized, sincere, thoughtful or humane . . . Savviness is that quality of being shrewd, practical, hyper-informed, perceptive, ironic, 'with it', and unsentimental in all things political. And what is the truest mark of savviness? Winning, of course! Or knowing who the winners are." See J. Rosen, "Why Political Coverage is Broken", *PressThink,* 26 August 2011.

20 H. Fairlie, "Press Against Politics" (1976), in J. McCarter (ed.), *Bite the Hand That Feeds You: Essays and Provocations* (Yale University Press, 2009), p. 277.

21 I. Murdoch, *The Sovereignty of Good* (Routledge & Kegan Paul, 1970), p. 52; I. Murdoch, *Metaphysics as a Guide to Morals* (Chatto & Windus, 1992), p. 463.

22 S. Weil, "The Iliad, or The Poem of Force" in S. Miles (ed.), *An Anthology (Penguin, 2005), p. 194.*

23 I am drawing here extremely selectively on a longer, more considered argument concerning the nature of contempt and its effect on democratic politics, which will appear in *On Contempt* (Melbourne University Press, forthcoming 2021).

24 I. Kant, *The Metaphysics of Morals, in Practical Philosophy*, transl. and ed. M.J. Gregor, The Cambridge Edition of the Works of Immanuel Kant (Cambridge University Press, 1996), pp. 582-3. George Eliot, that other great nineteenth-century moral philosopher, similarly warned against the dangers of "ridiculous" persons entering representative vocations (the particular role she has in mind here is the clergy, though it clearly translates across into representative politics—just think of the disappointed political ambitions of the ludicrous Arthur Brooke) because by doing so "we set men's minds to the tune of contempt": G. Eliot, *Middlemarch: A Study of Provincial Life* (Vintage, 2007), p. 429.

25 Kant, p. 582.

26 Fairlie, pp. 275-77.

27 *Ibid.*, pp. 273-4, 276.

28 J. Dewey, "Creative Democracy —The Task Before Us" in J.A. Boydston (ed.), *The Later Works of John Dewey, 1925–1953; Volume 14: 1939–1941* (Southern Illinois University Press, 2008), p. 227.

29 Dewey, "Democratic Ends Need Democratic Methods for Their Realization," in *Later Works*, Volume 14, p. 368.

30 Kateb, pp. 37, 40.

31 Sophia Rosenfeld connects democracy's virtue of "always providing for the possibility of second chances" to what she calls democracy's "particular vision of truth": "Democracy's great advantage is not a question of the empirical outcomes it generates . . . Rather, it is that we can never be certain we've got it right, and that's okay. New information or new knowledge can, at any point, potentially lead to new plans with new people at the helm. Moreover, knowing this is vital. For it is only if we can imagine moral and epistemological progress—that is, progress away from lies and propaganda and toward a truer view of reality, however elusive—that we can begin to rectify the gaps . . . between democratic ideals and the world in which we actually live and operate now." S. Rosenfeld, *Democracy and Truth: A Short History* (University of Pennsylvania Press, 2018), pp. 174-5.

32 H. Arendt, *The Promise of Politics*, ed. J. Kohn (Schocken Books, 2005), p. 196. See Montesquieu, *The Spirit of the Laws,* transl. A.M. Cohler, B.C. Miller and H.S. Stone (Cambridge University Press, 1989), pp. 21-30.

33 S. Cavell, "What Becomes of Things on Film?" in *Themes Out of School: Effects and Causes* (University of Chicago Press, 1984), p. 180.

34 I'll confess that I find the valorisation of Bradbury's novel, in particular, to be astonishing for the lack of self-awareness it suggests. After all, our digital era of unrestrained mass publication and instantaneous distribution—which has saturated our lives with written words in a manner and to a degree heretofore

unimaginable—has at the same time given rise to what can only be called a form of moral illiteracy, an epidemic of callow unresponsiveness to all but the basest, least exacting forms of communication, each one clambering for attention within Facebook's debauched empire of 'likes'.

35 S. Moyn, "The Trouble with Comparisons", *New York Review of Books*, 19 May 2020.

36 Dewey, "Creative Democracy", p. 226.

37 R. Gaita, "The Intelligentsia in the Age of Trump: Reflections on Truth and Truthfulness", *Meanjin Quarterly,* 2017, Vol. 76(3), p. 48.

38 S. Cavell, *The Senses of Walden,* expanded edn (University of Chicago Press, 1981), pp. 81-2.

Index